# Practicing the Prayer of St. Francis

# Practicing the Prayer of St. Francis

PATRICK ALLEN

WIPF & STOCK · Eugene, Oregon

PRACTICING THE PRAYER OF ST. FRANCIS

Wipf & Stock
An Imprint of Wipf and Stock Publishers
199 W. 8th Ave., Suite 3
Eugene, OR 97401

www.wipfandstock.com

PAPERBACK ISBN: 978-1-6667-5285-4
HARDCOVER ISBN: 978-1-6667-5286-1
EBOOK ISBN: 978-1-6667-5287-8

08/29/22

This book is dedicated to my wife, Lori, whose life constantly calls me to a more personal demonstration of my love for God and neighbor and a more intimate relationship with Christ. Simply put, I am a better Christian for it, and I truly believe this book is better for it, too.

For me, it all comes down to this:

Life is messy, but God is faithful.

# Contents

# Preface

I HADN'T WRITTEN SINCE I submitted the manuscript for *Love at Its Best When Church Is a Mess* in early February 2020, not a word. I usually take some time off before focusing my efforts on another writing project. Honestly, producing a manuscript that offers something more than spiritual chitchat, something that reflects my desire to live intentionally in such a way as to love both God and neighbor as if my life depended on it, something that shares my longing to be an authentic follower of Jesus as I make my way home, and something that is helpful and encouraging to others who desire to do the same—that kind of writing bids something from you long before it sees the light of day, so taking some time off before beginning another prolonged project made perfect sense. It was a form of self-care.

But this pause was different for two significant reasons. First, since I started writing seriously seven years ago, I have always had a list of "next projects" or at least a long list of writing ideas. My problem was always deciding what projects to undertake next and how to cull the list of interesting ideas to a manageable few. This time, however, there were no next big ideas, no energy, nothing. My idea list had dried up like an old leaf. There was absolutely nothing of interest to me, nothing that grabbed my attention or invited me to take another writing journey. It wasn't that I had writer's block. It wasn't that I couldn't write—I didn't want to write, and I could only hope that one day I would wake up wanting to write again, eager to lean into the task at hand.

You may have already surmised that the second significant factor was 2020, the year the pandemic made its way into all our lives and disrupted any sense of normality. Even though I am retired, it disrupted my life, too, in ways known and unknown, remembered and forgotten. While it may seem that diving into the deep water of a book project would have been a wonderful way to cope with the worry and disruption of the pandemic, it was just the opposite for me. I was somehow frozen in place—and fixed in time. Then, the social unrest in the aftermath of the killing of George Floyd and the political turmoil of an election year after three and a half years of political disruption just piled on. And here in the Northwest, we were literally surrounded by wildfires, unable to even leave our homes for two weeks as the skies turned an angry shade of orange and brown. To leave home was to risk your life! During all of that, I felt unable to be an encouragement to others. Honestly, my tank was empty, and I was simply trying to figure out how to survive in some meaningful way, in *any* meaningful way.

After nine months, a small miracle happened. Thankfully, the wildfires were finally out (for that year), although the devastation visited on so many who lost their homes, their livelihoods, and their communities remains. And there was still social and political unrest to be sure. So, what happened? On Tuesday evenings, my little church decided to offer a short, simple, socially distanced Word and Table service outdoors under the driveway awning in the parking lot; these services come in various forms but usually consist of a short devotional, the passing of the peace, and communion. Of course, it was good to see some familiar faces after so many months apart, and as part of one service we prayed together the familiar prayer of St. Francis. Now, I've heard and read this prayer many times, but this time it was different. It was as if the Holy Spirit said to me, "Patrick, this could be your next writing project." In my usual way of receiving instruction, I responded, "Seriously? I don't think so!" but I couldn't get away from the power of the message of this prayer, even during a pandemic, perhaps especially during a terrible pandemic year.

I could see that the prayer did not shy away from reality. Hatred, injury, doubt, despair, darkness, and sadness were named, but it asked that we *sow* love, pardon, faith, hope, light, and joy just the same. It acknowledged that self-seeking and self-serving are always with us, but asked that we *seek* to console, understand, and love others instead. And the prayer ended with the spiritual insight that as we make a practice of these things, we *see* that things come full circle. We receive when we give, we are pardoned even as we offer forgiveness, and as we die to a life of self-seeking, self-promoting, and self-serving, we are born to something eternal, something new. The working title came to me: *Practicing the Prayer of St. Francis.* I began to realize that this wasn't simply a prayer to be prayed, but a prayer to be practiced, to be lived out each day, even as the pandemic raged on and after it has been tamed, too. It is a prayer for all of life, a prayer to sow, seek, and see the goodness of God at work in this world and in our lives, and to participate in that work as best we can. I wanted to write about the Prayer of St. Francis to help others think about sowing, seeking, and seeing each day, regardless of the color of the skies. My motivation returned, and the energy flowed again.

My prayer is that this book will send you on a journey of faith, sustained by hope and nurtured by God's love as we, all of us, make our way home. At the end of the day, we don't just pray prayers, we practice them, we live them, and when we do, we are shaped even as we hope to shape the world around us by loving God and neighbor with everything we have.

*Deo gratias.*

PATRICK ALLEN
Newberg, Oregon
May 1, 2022

# Introduction

INSTRUMENTAL LIVING: *"LORD, MAKE me an instrument of your peace."* So begins what is now known as the Prayer of St. Francis. Born Giovanni di Pietro di Bernardone in the early twelfth century, Francis of Assisi embraced the idea of being an instrument of God's peace seriously. So much so that he traveled to Egypt in 1219 in an attempt to convert the Sultan, Al-Kamil, to Christianity in hopes of ending the horrific carnage of the Crusades. The Sultan was indeed willing to negotiate a peace settlement, but converting to Christianity was simply a step too far. I wonder if our own preconceived, nonnegotiable ideas of what the proper outcome must look like preclude other hopeful and helpful possibilities. Perhaps if we truly desire to be instruments used by God, we need to learn to play more than just one tune. Hopefully, this book will provide a few new songs for all of us.

It is a profound prayer to ask God to make you an instrument, crafted and tuned to be used for a purpose not of your own choosing but of God's. It is a humble prayer, a vulnerable prayer, and a risky prayer, too. Letting your life, all of it—your hopes, dreams, talents, abilities, opportunities, and resources—be used is to be "all in." It is a spiritual journey of a lifetime, and like Abraham who "obeyed and went, even though he didn't know where he was going" (Heb 11:8), we will have no idea where such a bold prayer will take us either. To me, that's part of the adventure of following Jesus. And along the way, we get to choose how we will journey—as tourists, travelers, or pilgrims. Throughout this book, I believe that you will come to see that when it comes to instrumental living, I have pilgrimage in mind.

And I think the peace that St. Francis had in mind was not simply a peaceful veneer, a thin line in the sand, or a shaky truce between hate and love, injury and pardon, doubt and faith, despair and hope, or darkness and light. Rather, I believe that he was thinking of shalom. He had in mind harmony, wholeness, tranquility, and justice—even a sense of delight in God and with life in God as it should be. That's a much bigger task on a much bigger playing field, and to ask God to make you an instrument of that kind of peace is to ask for the highest calling I can think of, and it will take all we have to offer—and more. Thankfully, we begin the prayer by asking God to do what only God can do. We want to be an instrument to sow, seek, and see shalom, but we do so in the loving care of the master creator and sustainer. An instrument does not make itself. As always, God does the heavy lifting. Our calling is to play a new song.

But let me be clear. This is not a happy, happy, happy Sunday morning worship kind of commitment. This is a passionate desire to be an instrument of God's peace, to go deep, and it isn't always a cakewalk. In fact, it rarely is. When Ignatius, bishop of Antioch, was arrested in the early second century and escorted by a squad of ten Roman soldiers to Rome, he knew that things would not end well. He would be tortured for profane pleasure and ultimately killed, yet he uttered these profound words: "Now I begin to be a disciple."[1]

Obviously, I hope and pray that none of us will be subjected to torture and death as we put this prayer into practice, but I do believe that when we work to sow shalom in fields of hate, injury, doubt, despair, darkness, and sadness, and seek to lay aside our own pride and self-seeking for the sake of others, it can be a lonely and sometimes painful process. Yet, it is in these trying times, shaping times, that we can also say, "Now I begin to be a disciple." Let's go deep together and trust that the God who made water flow from a rock for a people in exile and lost in the desert will do the same for each of us.

## THE ORGANIZATION OF THIS BOOK

This book is organized into three parts around three powerful verbs in St. Francis's prayer: *Sowing*, *Seeking*, and *Seeing*. In Part I: *Sowing*, we investigate what it means to sow seeds of peace and what practices we can employ to bring about a fruitful harvest, knowing full well that the Lord of the Harvest is always with us. In Part II: *Seeking*, we consider several spiritual practices that will shape us as we strive to put others before ourselves, as hard as that can be for all of us at one time or another, or in my case, for most of the time. And finally, in Part III: *Seeing*, we meditate on what it means to remember God's goodness to us, why such memories are so important for our spiritual formation, and how expressions of gratitude can be a powerful spiritual discipline for all of us as we strive to make our way home.

Most chapters include a short meditation, a story or two, references to Scripture, suggestions for practicing what we pray, and questions for

1. Ignatius of Antioch, "Epistle of Ignatius," ch. 5.

reflection and discussion. Hopefully, this format will be beneficial for you, whether used for personal devotions or in a small group setting.

## MY HOPE AND PRAYER

My hope for this book is that it will lead all of us into a deeper understanding of what it means to pray in earnest, asking God to make us instruments of shalom, and give each of us some practical tools and disciplines for doing so. My prayer is that we take seriously the challenge left to us so long ago by St. Francis—to give hands and feet to our prayers and to practice what we pray. I believe we reach a turning point in our spiritual formation when we realize that praying is more about intentions and practices than it is about words, even though most of us are captivated by our own words. Honestly, I think that God in more interested in our actions. Let's practice the Prayer of St. Francis together. Now we begin to be disciples!

The Prayer of St. Francis
*Lord, make me an instrument of your peace.*
*Where there is hatred, let me sow love;*
*Where there is injury, pardon;*
*Where there is doubt, faith;*
*Where there is despair, hope;*
*Where there is darkness, light;*
*Where there is sadness, joy.*
*O Divine Master,*
*Grant that I may not so much seek*
*To be consoled as to console;*
*To be understood as to understand;*
*To be loved as to love.*
*For it is in giving that we receive;*
*It is in pardoning that we are pardoned;*
*And it is in dying that we are born to eternal life.*
*Amen.*[2]

2. "Franciscan and Other Prayers."

# PART I

## Sowing in Hard Soil

PLANTING SEEDS IS AN act of faith. Obviously, we have no ultimate control over the outcome, but sowing is a critical part of the process. Truly, we participate in one of the mysteries of life, acknowledging that we are junior partners in it all. Creating new life is way above our pay grade.

And sowing successfully in hard soil is simply hard to do. As any experienced gardener will tell you, extra work is required to prepare the soil, nourish the tender shoots, and tend to them as they take root and grow. And when they begin to bear fruit, even more care is required, especially when we pray to sow seeds of peace where there is hatred, injury, doubt, despair, darkness, and sadness. This is the hard soil of life. If we are to see our prayers bear fruit, we must be clear about what will be expected of us, committed to the process, and willing to dig in for the long haul.

The Prayer of St. Francis is a call to action. It is not a Sunday morning feel-good prayer. Rather, it is an everyday, roll-up-your-sleeves, and stick-with-it kind of undertaking. Hopefully, these next chapters will provide some perspectives and suggest some spiritual practices to help us as we sow the tender seeds of peace in the hardpan we find around us and in our own lives, too. We'll begin with one of the hardest soils I can think of—hatred.

# 1

# Sowing Love Where There Is Hatred

## *The Practice of Inclusion*

Love recognizes no barriers. It jumps hurdles, leaps fences, penetrates walls to arrive at its destination full of hope.

—MAYA ANGELOU

## INTRODUCTION

Must we start with hatred? Can't we ease into this sowing-seeds-of-peace prayer just a bit by first addressing doubt, sadness, even despair? Hatred is the hardpan of soils, virtually impervious to water and most other nutrients, so sowing love there is really difficult, but perhaps it is the place most in need of our attention and care. "Where there is hatred, let me sow love," we pray. So, let's put some hands and feet to our prayers.

There are, of course, many forms of hatred all around us, and if we're honest, in us, too. Here I am not thinking of the overt and utterly horrible instances and outcroppings of hatred—racism, genocide, torture, violence, murder, and war, to name just a few. No, here I want our prayers to sow love in fields of hatred that are personal, honest, and closer to home. I want us to deal with issues that we live with each day but often do not even notice.

Others have and will continue to deal with the "big" hatred issues mentioned above. Surely, they beg and need the world's attention, but so do the little thoughts and actions that we promote in our own neighborhoods and churches. If hatred is defined as extreme dislike, ill will, resentment, prejudiced hostility, and animosity, then we must face the fact that hatred is at work where we worship, work, and live.

## Hatred under the Radar

I want us to examine two kinds of hatred that slip under the radar: exclusion and intolerance. These two may surprise you. You may be asking: Are they really acts of hatred or are they simply human shortcomings or irritations we must put up with? I have come to believe that acts of exclusion and intolerance are serious spiritual matters because they isolate, insulate, and divide one neighbor from another, and often one Christian from another, too. And as they do, we are all diminished and demeaned. That can't be good. We'll address these under-the-radar forms of hatred before turning our attention to practices we can employ as we sow love in the hardest of soils, but first let me share two short stories—both personal experiences.

### The Friendship Circle

When my wife was invited to lead the music for a new contemporary service at a very upscale church in a very upscale part of San Diego, I decided to tag along. I often drove my old pickup. It looked out of place in the parking lot full of luxury automobiles and even a limo or two. The contemporary service was scheduled early on Sunday morning, followed by the traditional service complete with a choir in robes, an organ, and a full orchestra. The contemporary service used a piano, two guitars, and a drum set. It was quite a cultural contrast for this affluent church, and attendance at the contemporary service was sparse. Between services, there was a forty-five-minute fellowship time on the patio, complete with a table stacked high with fruits and snacks, and a wonderful view of the Pacific Ocean.

The pastor announced during the contemporary service that a large circle, called the Friendship Circle, could be found painted on the patio, and if you were new to the church, you were to stand in the circle. Someone would welcome you and help you find your way. So, after the service I went and stood in the Friendship Circle for almost a half hour, but no one talked to me—no one. I repeated my efforts the next two Sundays with no human contact. Finally, late on my third week's attempt, I saw someone approaching me. "Great," I thought, "I'll finally get to meet someone." The person smiled at me and asked, "Could you move over a bit? You are kind of blocking the direct line to the snacks." That was it. I moved over "a bit" and those in line for the snacks happily talked and joked with each other as they filed by me. I finally walked away and never went back. The message was clear—I wasn't welcome there. Although the message of dislike and prejudice was subtle, I received it loud and clear. It was exclusion under the radar.

## Associate Membership

My wife and I were attending our first business meeting at another church. We had attended for almost a year, and helped out with music on a regular basis. I was even asked to preach one Sunday morning, but we had never attended the monthly business meeting where the elected committees met to conduct church business and make important financial decisions. These meetings were held after church. All were welcome, we were told, and it was clear that most of the influential members of the congregation were in attendance. I was being considered for membership on one of the committees, so we thought that it would be good to see what went on at the meeting before I attended as an elected committee member.

The meeting agenda had two main items: what public statement, if any, should be made about homosexuality, and what was the church's position on the use of alcohol by its members. As you might expect, the conversation was tense, and it went on for a long time. Finally, a church leader stood up and said that he felt the Bible was entirely clear about homosexuality and the church should be, too. There could be no disagreement about that! Honestly, I don't know if it was because I had spent my entire adult life working on university campuses where I enjoyed rich dialogue with colleagues, even in disagreement, perhaps especially in disagreement, or if it was my own bent to provide an alternative view, but I pointed out a few flaws in the leader's argument and his interpretation of Scripture. That didn't sit well with the leader. Apparently, one of the unwritten rules of the business meeting was that no one should contradict anything said by the leadership. I didn't know that, but I did heard whispers a few rows behind me: "He's soft on gays!"

Although it was difficult, I remained quiet throughout the rest of the meeting—well, throughout most of it. The conversation turned to the use of alcohol by members, and another leader stood up and proudly told the story of a couple who wanted to join the church, but it caused problems for the membership committee because they owned and operated a local winery. It wasn't entirely clear, but they assumed that they also drank some of the fruits of their labors, which was probably an accurate assumption. The leader went on to say that even though there was no prohibition concerning the use of alcohol in the criteria for church membership, the committee felt that they needed to take a moral stand. So, they refused to let the couple join the church as full members, but they did offer them associate membership. It wasn't entirely clear what associate membership entailed, but what was clear was that they would not to be considered for membership on any church committee or for any leadership position in the church. Obviously, they were viewed as outsiders, as second-class members, and their lifestyle would not be condoned. They were hurt, but in a loving Christian way, of course.

It was all I could do to keep from yelling, but I did comment with all the restraint that I could muster: "What an interesting way to deal with this issue. I'm glad to know that Jesus could be an associate member here."

As you might expect, my comment was not well-received. In fact, it was met with stone-cold silence. Again, I had violated one of the unwritten rules of the business meeting, but to this day, I'm not sure which rule it was. There were a lot of unwritten rules. What I am sure of is that during the next week my name was removed from the committee election ballot. Clearly, I was neither wanted nor welcome to serve in any capacity at the church. I guess that I was an associate member, too. My questions and perspectives were not welcome.

What these two stories have in common is silence in one form or another, but it is not a holy silence. Of course, silence can lead to times of helpful meditation, reflection, and prayer, but the silence in these stories demonstrates a form of intolerance that leads to exclusion—forms of ill-will that are rightly called hatred. I know that sounds harsh, but if we're going to sow seeds of love in the hardpan of hatred right where we live and worship, we must recognize and name these behaviors for what they are, especially when they are practiced in Christian community.

## Exclusion

You can tell a lot about a church by where the line is drawn between "us and them," and particularly so when the line is drawn at the front door of the church building. Those literally on the inside are good, while everyone else is suspect. They are outsiders—misguided, mistaken, mistrusted, unwelcome, even dangerous, and must be avoided or silenced or both. When this happens, suspicion leads to ill-will, and ill-will leads to the practice of shunning and exclusion, not too subtle forms of hatred.

As one reads through the Bible, the arc of the narrative bends toward inclusion. We first see God's covenant with one person, Abraham, as he sets out for a land that was to become his inheritance. Later, we see God's covenant with a people, the children of Israel, as they fled the tyranny of Egypt and wandered their way to the promised land. I heard one pastor say that God not only had to get the children of Israel out of Egypt, but God had to get Egypt out of his people, too. I think that process is still going on within each of us.

Jesus' ministry was more inclusive still, associating with Samaritan women, dining with tax collectors, healing lepers and other outcasts, even the children of Roman soldiers, and forgiving the sins of prostitutes. He was concerned with embrace and inclusion, not ritualistic purity, and he took a good deal of heat for it from the establishment. In due time, it cost him his life. Even when speaking of his impending death, he was inclusive: "And I, when I am lifted up from the earth, will draw *all* people to myself" (John 12:32). That's all people—all.

The coming of the Holy Spirit was inclusive, too. According to Luke, "When the day of Pentecost came, they were *all* together in one place" (Acts 2:1). Note that word again—all. "*All* of them were filled with the Holy Spirit . . . Parthians, Medes and Elamites; residents of Mesopotamia, Judea and Cappadocia, Pontus, and Asia, Phrygia and Pamphylia, Egypt and the parts of Libya near Cyrene; visitors from Rome (both Jews and converts to Judaism); Cretans and Arabs—we hear them declaring the wonders of God in their own tongues!" (Acts 2:4, 9–11).

Peter and Paul preached and pushed and practiced this same inclusive arc as fledgling Christian communities began to form, not only in Jerusalem but in cities across the Mediterranean as well—and not only among Jews who faithfully kept the rules and rituals of worship at their local synagogue, but among gentiles, too. It was another grand inclusive embrace, one of the major themes of the Bible. Yet, exclusion so often slides under the radar because we don't see it, and because we don't see it, we don't speak out against it or change the way we live. If we desire to sow seeds of love where there is hatred, practicing inclusion is a good place to start.

## Intolerance

Intolerance and exclusion are not the same thing, but they are cousins. While exclusion keeps others away who are not like us or do not worship like us or do not practice their faith like us (outsiders), intolerance is aimed at insiders, particularly those who have sincere doubts and honest questions about the prevailing theology of the church or denomination or movement, how the Bible is read and interpreted, the role of the leader, women in ministry, baptism or prophesy or speaking in tongues or holy living. I could name many more, but I think you get my point. Every Christian community has theological stances. That's not the issue. The issue is whether and to what extent there are opportunities to not only explore "what *we* believe" but also to share any questions or concerns that you may have, to share what *I* believe. Are there opportunities for open discourse? Is it encouraged or are such questions unwelcome, viewed as signs of disbelief, disloyalty, or a lack of faith? If they are unwelcome, intolerance is lurking just under the radar.

When you are told "it's our way or the highway," I suggest you look for the highway, particularly when you have serious reservations or moral concerns about "our way." No fellowship should ever ask you to check your brains or your moral compass at the door to gain membership. Intolerance can produce a deep sense of cohesion among its members but sadly at great personal and spiritual cost, not only for those who are no longer welcomed but also for those thick in the group. Exclusion guards the front door while intolerance uses the back door to push those out who do not toe the party line.

## Spiritual Blindness

Indifference, of course, is not always a bad thing. To be indifferent about the results of the Super Bowl or the National Dog Show or the Nobel Prize for Literature is a matter of personal interest and taste. Surely, we can't be interested in everything. And we can be indifferent about the worship team's music selection or the color of the carpet in the vestibule or how the Christmas decorations are displayed in the sanctuary, too, but in my experience, there is more stir about these kinds of "church issues" than about the homeless who live near the church or the growing unemployment and poverty we see close to home. That's where indifference is troublesome. Since Jesus said that loving God and loving our neighbor as ourselves was the way to eternal life (Luke 10:25–28), clearly a lack of concern or interest in the plight of others is wrong. Indifference leads inevitably to a lack of action. It is like driving by a burning house and not stopping to help or calling 911. We don't even recognize that someone needs our help! This type of indifference is a form of social blindness.

And when we don't see how exclusion and intolerance are practiced in our faith community, how *we* practice or permit exclusion and intolerance, then we who claim Christ are spiritually blind, too. Spiritual blindness makes it easy to come to worship each Sunday, sing loudly, say a hearty Amen to the sermon, and then go out for lunch with friends without being challenged to see differently—to live out our faith differently. Spiritual blindness leaves everyone diminished, especially us, because what we care about will shape us—for good or for ill. What we overlook will shape us, too.

I realize that this section on hatred under the radar is tough sledding for all of us, and it was hard for me to write, too. However, I believe that if we are to practice the Prayer of St. Francis seriously, we must start close to home, right where we live and worship. We must deal with the things that tend to slide by, recognizing them for what they are and for the violence they visit upon those around us, and upon each of us, too—as subtle forms of hatred.

But we need not end in despair! Honestly, the Prayer of St. Francis is a hopeful, grace-filled prayer. We will turn first to a story from the Bible for insight and direction. Then, I'll offer some spiritual practices to help us faithfully sow love in the hardpan we find close to home. When we pray *"Lord, make me an instrument of your peace. Where there is hatred, let me sow love,"* it is not a prayer prayed in vain or without resources to accomplish the task. Let's prepare to sow!

## SCRIPTURE

If there was ever a social and religious outcast, it was Zacchaeus the tax collector. He was a chief tax collector in Jericho, the hub for the production and distribution of balsam, so there was money in Jericho—and Zacchaeus had money, too. He made his living by extorting local taxpayers, asking for more than the tax code demanded and then skimming off the difference, and accepting bribes to reduce a tax bill or two. Zacchaeus was a Jew, perhaps a devout Jew, but since he worked for the Romans, he was seen as an outcast and treated as a traitor. No respectable Jew would have anything to do with him.

All this, and Zacchaeus was a short man, too. So short, in fact, that when he heard that Jesus was passing through Jericho, he couldn't see over the crowd. He climbed a nearby sycamore tree to get a better view. That's where the story gets interesting. When Jesus looked up and saw him clinging to a tree branch, he said, "Zacchaeus, come down immediately. I must stay at your house today" (Luke 19:5). Now, it is not clear how Jesus spotted Zacchaeus amid all the commotion that accompanied his arrival in Jericho in the first place, or how he knew his name, or why he wanted to delay his journey to have a meal with Jericho's chief social and religious outcast. But what is clear is that he did—and the locals didn't like it a bit! "He has gone to be the guest of a sinner," they muttered to themselves, but loudly enough for Jesus and everyone else to hear them (Luke 19:7). Zacchaeus was so moved by his meeting with Jesus that he promised to give away half of his possessions and repay anyone he had cheated with four times the amount, which was in keeping with the Old Testament prescription for making such things right (Exod 22; Lev 6). To be honest, we don't know if he ever did make things right, but it seems that his earnest declaration was more than enough for Jesus. The story ends with Jesus telling Zacchaeus that salvation had come to his house that day, and he added, "This man, too, is a son of Abraham" (Luke 19:9).

What a powerful story of sowing love in the hardpan of hatred. Several things are worth mentioning here. First, Jesus was just passing through Jericho but changed his plans when he saw Zacchaeus. How often do we rush through our days trying to get somewhere and back home by dark? Would we be willing to change our plans to have a meal with an outcast? And would we even see Zacchaeus sitting in that tree and take the time to find out his name, or would we be focused on those cozying up to us and cheering us on?

Second, I'm pretty sure that Jesus knew that he would be criticized for having a meal with a local tax collector, scorned even. He could hear the muttering, but it seems that he didn't really care. He was on a mission. So, how about us? How do we deal with criticism? Do we have a mission that would override the mutterings of our friends and neighbors?

Finally, Jesus told his listeners that Zacchaeus was a son of Abraham, too. He was not one of "them"—he was one of "us," even before he jumped through a string of hoops to demonstrate the sincerity of his repentance. I wonder what we would have expected Zacchaeus to do before we welcomed him back into our church. Would we recognize that the tax collector sitting in the tree is just as important as the one leading the procession down the center isle or sitting at the head table or playing in the worship team? There's a lesson here for all of us who claim Christ.

## PRACTICING THE PRAYER OF ST. FRANCIS

Sowing love sounds easy, but it's not, especially if we are sowing where hatred abounds—even subtle forms of hatred such as exclusion and intolerance. Let me suggest several ways that we can put the Prayer of St. Francis into practice, and I believe that as we do we will be shaped and formed in the image of Christ. As it turns out, even if we have little noticeable impact on the behavior of those around us, these practices will change us. Perhaps that is what St. Francis had in mind all along. I'll let you decide.

## Stop, Look, and Listen

Just as Jesus saw Zacchaeus and stopped, changing his plans for the day, might we do the same? Let's just *Stop* and take an exclusion assessment. You can do this alone, but I think it is more instructive and helpful if you include a small group of thoughtful, faithful friends. Ask these questions: Who are the outsiders among us, those hanging from a tree branch hoping for a glimpse of Jesus? What are their names? How might we practice inclusion and acceptance right where we live? What would be several small first steps to take as we strive to love our neighbors as ourselves? Write them down.

*Look and Listen*—Jesus saw Zacchaeus amid all the hullabaloo and ballyhoo as he made his way through Jericho. He hadn't planned to stop, but he did. How can we do the same as we make our way through the hullabaloo and ballyhoo of our daily lives? It starts with intention. Take just a few minutes at the beginning of each day and ask God to give you "eyes to see" and "ears to hear" subtle acts of hatred as they play out around you. Then, be vigilant, keeping careful watch for instances and opportunities to step in and practice what we pray.

A good place to start is to speak to those who are so often overlooked— the gas station attendant, the grocery store checker, the restaurant server, the coffee barista, and the landscaper, to name just a few—persons you cross paths with each day. Look them in the eyes, talk to them, learn their names, and get to know some of their story. It is a way of saying, "I see you." And when they are hurting, they may just seek you out. If they do, the task of sowing love becomes sheer joy.

## Show Up and Get Involved

Social science research tells us that lives are not changed by words. It is a temptation to point out all the subtle forms of hatred we see around us and tell others what they should do to correct their ways. However, actions speak much louder than words. Scolding simply entrenches attitudes and behaviors. Rather, it is our own presence, especially when vested over time in relationships, that changes minds and hearts. We must earn the right to speak, and we do so by seeing, listening, and then showing up—again and again and again. When we pray to sow love where there is hatred, it calls us to be a faithful presence each day. Our lives will speak for themselves.

## Practice Patience and Persistence

"Steadfast love" is a translation from the Hebrew word *chesed*, found over two hundred times in the Hebrew Bible and over one hundred times in the Psalms alone. It has also been translated as "loving-kindness," "mercy," and "loyalty." I think you can add "patience" and "persistence" to that list, too. God is the God-of-the-Patient-Wait. God's kindness and mercy are steadfast and long-suffering. Ours can be, too.

Why is this important? The Prayer of St. Francis is not a quick-fix prayer, a one-and-done recitation. Rather, it is a prayer of commitment, of long-suffering, of steadfast love. When we ask God to help us sow seeds of love in fields of hatred, we must be in it for the long haul. When the Christian fellowship in Corinth wrote to the apostle Paul and asked for guidance to see their way through the big mess they were in, mostly of their own doing, he told them that they needed to love each other—with a love that was patient and kind (1 Cor 13:4a). I think his advice is good for all of us today. When we pray the Prayer of St. Francis, it is a call to patient and persistent involvement with kindness—spiritual practices that challenge us even as they change us.

## A FINAL THOUGHT

We will end as we began. Planting seeds is an act of faith, and sowing love where there is hatred may be the most daunting task that we will ever face, especially when acts of hatred (we discussed exclusion and intolerance) can so easily slip by under the radar or be excused as simply shabby behavior. Sadly, these acts hurt others, and they diminish us, too. One might wonder if the seeds of love can even grow in such hardpan. At times, I know I have.

But we cannot forget the power of love. On one hot summer's day at a Memphis public swimming pool, a young boy drifted into the deep end of the pool and began to flail. He was not a good swimmer. He panicked and screamed for help. Suddenly, his mother jumped into the pool and pushed and shoved her son to safety, but, exhausted, she sank in the water and didn't come up. She drowned saving her son's life. Now I ask you: What in the world would cause someone who was deathly afraid of the water and unable to swim to willingly jump into the deep end of a swimming pool? Only one thing—love.

When we desire to sow love in fields of hatred, we do so with confidence—not in our own abilities of persuasion, but with the knowledge that "*love recognizes no barriers. It jumps hurdles, leaps fences, penetrates walls to arrive at its destination full of hope.*"[1] It is the most powerful thing in the world.

## QUESTIONS FOR REFLECTION AND DISCUSSION

1. Have you ever been treated as an outsider, as one of "them"? How did it make you feel, and what did you do about it? Did it change your attitude, behavior, or theology in any significant way? If so, how?

2. Have you ever been the one doing the excluding? What were the circumstances, and what would you do differently now?

3. When you think about your own faith community, how would you rate its openness to questions and discussions about matters of faith and practice? How strong are its expectations for adherence to core theological beliefs or communal practices? What happens when differences of theology and interpretation arise? Where is the line beyond which differences in opinion are unwelcome?

4. When there is heartbreak in the church, how might you reach out to those who are suffering in silence?

5. Have you witnessed the power of love in action? Who has expressed it to you, and how might you express it forward?

The Prayer of St. Francis
*Lord, make me an instrument of your peace.*
*Where there is hatred, let me sow love;*

1. Angelou, "Love Recognizes No Barriers."

# 2

# Sowing Pardon Where There Is Injury

*The Practice of Forgiveness*

Forgiveness does not change the past, but it does enlarge the future.
—PAUL BOESE

## INTRODUCTION

Before we talk about pardon, we need to talk about injuries. We all have experienced them, and some of us carry some of them with us even now. The memories are real, and they can be painful, too. Just when we think we are past all of it, whatever "it" is, even the simplest comment or the sight of a certain one going into the grocery store can bring up a rush of painful memories, resentment, even self-doubt. In one sense, of course, we are all cracked pots. No one gets through this world unscathed. We're all wounded. Everyday life leaves its mark on all of us, but some injuries don't seem to heal, won't go away. And at some time or another, we all come up short. Sadly, we hurt other people, too, and often they are the ones we love the most—or are supposed to love the most.

In the following section, we'll look at three different kinds of injuries: injuries we cause, injuries we encounter, and injuries we carry. As we will see, how we sow pardon depends a good deal on the type of injury we are dealing with. There isn't a one-size-fits-all universal response to injury. And as it turns out, like grace, pardon comes in various forms, too (see 1 Pet 4:10).

## The Injuries We Cause—Seeking Forgiveness

Let's start with the kind of injuries we don't want to talk about, or even think about—the injuries we cause. How do we sow pardon when we are the ones who did the injuring in the first place? To start with, it isn't easy, and we won't always be successful. In some cases, we are not even welcome to try. This reality must be faced, remembering that we don't have the power to force a reconciliation, and it would not be advisable even if we could.

So, where do we start when we recognize that we are the injuring party? I believe we start with three simple acts: saying we are sorry, admitting we were wrong, and asking for forgiveness. Simple acts, indeed, yet so hard to do, but when we do so with sincerity and humility, we are on the right road, wherever it may finally lead.

Honestly, saying you're sorry in an insincere way can be quite easy to do. When one of my brothers and I would get into a tiff at home, my mother would make us face each other, say that we were sorry, and shake hands. "Sorry, said sorry," we would say in the most insincere way possible without even looking at each other, but that didn't get us off the hook. "Say it again, and this time mean it!" she told us, so we did. Over time, I think we did learn to mean it. I guess in this case, practice does make perfect.

In my capacity as a university provost, I had to deal from time to time with faculty disputes—sometimes professional, but most of the time personal. They were the worst to work through. On more than one occasion, someone would say, "I'm sorry you feel that way." Of course, it was a start, but a poor one. Saying one is sorry about how the other person feels is a thinly veiled attempt to point out that the other person took the whole matter wrongly or was simply too sensitive for their own good. And if the truth be told, "I'm sorry you took it that way" usually meant that the speaker wasn't sorry for anything they did—not anything! They were just embarrassed that they were called to the provost's office. Obviously, that's no way to sow seeds of pardon where there is injury.

However, saying you're sorry is the right place to start, but you have to mean it. Most of us are equipped with a kind of interpersonal radar that detects when someone is just blowing smoke or trying to excuse their actions. Such insincerity is easily detectable, and it spoils the gesture. But when you look someone in the eyes or write them a personal note expressing regret for your actions, intentional or unintentional, a simple "I'm sorry" goes a long way down the road to reestablishing a right relationship.

A long way down the road, indeed, but saying "I'm sorry" is the starting point, not the end of the road. To say "I'm sorry" is to express how you feel, an emotion; to say "I was wrong" is to admit poor behavior, that you did something wrong. I think this is perhaps the hardest thing to admit. You not only feel sorry for the situation, but you admit that you were wrong to behave the way you did or that you did something hurtful or wrong. This is hard, but I think when you bring together an expression of remorse with the admission that you behaved wrongly, the sincerity of your apology is magnified. It becomes real.

And the final step is to ask for forgiveness simply and humbly—"Will you forgive me?" Hopefully, the answer is yes, but sometimes the answer is no. Sometimes, instead of accepting your apology, they may give you a piece of their mind and show you the door. You humbly ask for forgiveness, but you get anger and hurt instead. That's ok—and understandable. Perhaps the timing was wrong, or the pain was too great. In such cases, time can be a healer. And sometimes your apology, no matter how earnestly and humbly offered, may never be accepted. That causes a memory and pain of a different kind, but you must remember and reconcile with the reality that it is up to you to apologize, admit that you were wrong, and ask for forgiveness; it is up to the other person to accept or reject your offering. It's on them, and regardless of their response, you have done what you knew to do to make amends.

Moving on in the face of an unaccepted apology, hoping to learn from your mistake, is terribly hard to do, but sometimes it is the only thing you can do. Often, when we look back at our lives, we see our failures lit up in bright lights. We carry a deep sense of regret and guilt. We wish we would have behaved differently. And even though we know that we are all broken pots in one way or another, we still carry shame about our own cracks, as if we were supposed to be perfect. Let's be honest; we're not. Fortunately, we are called to be faithful, not perfect. Sometimes the person who most needs your forgiveness is you. The question is—will *you* accept it? We have to trust the work of the Holy Spirit in others' lives, and in our own lives, too. It is an act of hope, an expression of grace.

## Injuries We Encounter—Offering Comfort

It's one thing to deal with the injuries we cause, but what about the injuries we encounter along the way? How do we sow pardon where there is injury when we learn about the injury after the fact, an injury that we had nothing to do with giving or receiving? Perhaps we just hear that someone was hurt, or a deep injury is shared with us as a friendship deepens. What do we do, and perhaps more importantly, what don't we do as we pray to sow pardon where there is injury?

First, it is important to keep a proper perspective: the injury didn't happen to us. We are not the victim, so we can't take on all the pain and suffering, no matter how unjust or hurtful the situation may be. Healing does not come because we get upset and angry, too. It is not about us. Our job is to calm the waters, not stir up the mud. A good strategy is to keep the spotlight on the injured person and off ourselves. Going on and on about how angry we are and how much sleep we are losing does nothing to address the injury and usually gets in the way of finding a way forward.

Secondly, try to avoid giving advice, particularly uninvited advice. I had a colleague at the university who would start yelling as soon as he saw me walking down Alumni Lane, even though we were some distance apart: "Dean Allen, Dean Allen, do you know what you should do?!" He always had advice for me. Honestly, I avoided Alumni Lane most days. Uninvited advice is a real pain. And when we know someone who is dealing with injury of one kind or another, particularly someone we care about, the grave temptation is to step in and say, "Do you know what you should do?!" Don't do it, please. It won't help. And even when someone asks for our advice, be very careful. More times than not, several carefully crafted questions better serve the situation than a litany of half-baked suggestions.

Thirdly, don't try to save the circus. It's not up to us to mediate, negotiate, or fix the situation. It is tempting to jump in and give someone a piece of our mind or attempt to bring the parties together or function as a go-between, but it rarely works out. More times than not, we just complicate an already painful situation and make the injured party a passive spectator. Remember, it's their circus. They don't work for us. Our role is to offer comfort.

So, how do we offer comfort? We can offer a meal, a hug, and a listening ear. We can ask good questions about how they feel, how they plan to move forward, and what they are learning about themselves and about God through this injury. We can say that we are sorry, really sorry. We can let them know that we will be praying for them daily, and then offer a prayer for them in their presence. And we can suggest a few simple spiritual practices like bookending each day, starting in the morning with the intention of seeing God at work and ending in the evening with a review of where the presence of the Holy Spirit was evident, or in every situation, especially painful and threatening situations, to simply repeat, "God is present." It is an old Ignatian practice that brings comfort and healing. I'm not sure how it works, but I know it does. And perhaps most importantly, we can simply sit with our injured friend and be still, saying nothing. It is a powerful form of comfort.

At the end of the day, when we encounter injury that is not of our own doing, we are not called to make the injury ours, take over the fight, or heal a friend. Rather, we are called to be present, to be patient, to be kind. We sow pardon by bringing comfort.

## Injuries We Carry—Longing for Healing

There is one more type of injury I want to discuss—the injuries we carry with us. At one time or another, most of us will be hurt by someone or caught up in a wounding situation. Some will be intentional, others unintentional, but we carry the hurt, nonetheless. And often there is no attempt at seeking forgiveness by the injuring party. Sometimes, it will not even be acknowledged that anyone was hurt, and at other times, we will be accused of grandstanding or urged to get over it and move on. How do we sow pardon where there is injury when we are the ones with the injury? Isn't it up to the other person to come to us, apologize, and ask for forgiveness? In a perfect world, perhaps, but the world is not perfect.

So, what do we do when we sincerely pray to be an instrument of God's peace by sowing pardon where there is injury, with our injury? If a sincere apology is offered, we need to summon all the grace and courage we can to accept it. This will not make the pain magically go away or restore everything to what it was. We do not have to act as if nothing happened, because something hurtful did happen. We can, however, accept the apology as an expression of our hope and trust in the healing power of God's presence. Doing so allows us to have agency in our own life instead of being a victim. The hurt will slowly fade, but it takes time—so take your time. In this case, time is the great healer.

And if no apology is extended, what then? I think we start with lament, by honestly and emotionally pouring out our hurt before God. This is exactly what Jesus did as he was being crucified. He didn't quote from Ps 23, "The Lord is my shepherd, I lack nothing . . ." (23:1), or Jer 29:11, "For I know the plans I have to you . . . ," although I'm certain that he was familiar with both. Rather, he lamented a portion from Ps 22:1, "My God, my God, why have you forsaken me?"

It is not just ok to lament; it is important to do so. We can tell God how we feel; God can take it. It is the first step on the long journey toward healing, and there is no reason to make the journey alone. Seek out a close friend, trusted spiritual advisor, or professional counselor. Take time to acknowledge the injury, look for small, positive steps to take to move forward, go at your own pace, and trust in God's grace, healing, and presence. It sounds simple, but it is one of the hardest journeys we will ever take. We work our way through our hurt and anger believing that God is working in us and through us, and when we get there, wherever there is, God is already there and at work, too. Healing comes as an act of faith in the goodness of God.

There is much more that can be said about injury and forgiveness, particularly as we strive to be faithful to God and forgiving of others and ourselves. We'll pick up this theme again in chapter 11. Suffice it here to say that when we sincerely pray to sow pardon where there is injury, it will require our very best—and then some. It is a prayer for forgiveness, for holiness, something we cannot achieve on our own. The good news is that we don't have to. As Jesus told his disciples, "I am the vine; you are the branches. If you remain in me and I in you, you will bear much fruit" (John 15:5). Our job is to remain in him and be the branches. That we can do. Thanks be to God.


## SCRIPTURE

It is difficult to read the Bible regularly without noticing that the repetition of words and events is prevalent throughout the text. Clearly, numbers were important for writers in biblical times, and some carried significant spiritual meaning. Take the number forty, for example. It often signified new life, new growth, transformation, or a change from one great task to another great task. We see this in the forty-day rain leading up to the great flood and Noah's epic journey (Gen 7:12). Moses fasted for forty days on Mount Sinai as he received the law (Deut 9:18). The Israelites wandered in the desert for forty years (see Numbers). Jesus went from his baptism to the wilderness to be tested for forty days before he began his ministry (Matt 4:1–11), and according to the writer of Acts, Jesus ascended into heaven forty days after his resurrection (Acts 1:9–12). The use of the number forty signified that these events were not just random, routine human happenings; they were significant, powerful, transformative, spiritual events in the lives of all involved.

The number three had added significance for biblical writers, too. When something was repeated three times, it often meant "pay attention, this is important!" And so were events that were repeated three times or occurred over three days. In the Hebrew Bible, think of the calling of Samuel. God called out to him three times in the middle of the night (1 Sam 3:4–10). In Isaiah's well-known vision in the year that King Uzziah died, he saw the seraphim calling to each other, "Holy, holy, holy is the Lord Almighty; the whole earth is full of his glory" (Isa 6:3). Note the word "holy" was repeated three times. It is not a casual description of God. Then there were three young men sent into Nebuchadnezzar's fiery furnace (Dan 3:12–30), Jonah spent three days and nights in the belly of a huge fish (Jonah 1:17), and in Scripture, there were three patriarchs: Abraham, Isaac, and Jacob (Exod 3:6).

The use and significance of the number three continues in the Gospels as well. Matthew reports that three magi arrived in Bethlehem soon after the birth of Jesus (Matt 2:1–12). On the night of his arrest, Jesus went to a private place of prayer in the garden of Gethsemane three times, and after his crucifixion he rose from the dead on the third day. Mark reports that three women visited Jesus' tomb (Mark 16:1), and according to John, Jesus appeared to his disciples three times after his resurrection (John 21:14). The significance of these events in the gospel story cannot be overstated.

One of the most familiar uses of the number three appears in the Gospels when Peter, insisting that he was ready to lay down his life for Jesus at any time, was told that he would deny Jesus three times before the sun rose the next morning—and he did before it did (Matt 26:34; Luke 22:34; John 13:38). Why three times? To me, it suggests that the writers were wanting to convey the seriousness of this denial. This was no simple mistake, a stumble, or an oversight on Peter's part. It was momentous. It was unthinkable. It was terribly sad. Remember, Jesus told Peter that he was to be the rock upon which the church would be built, and even the gates of hell couldn't prevail against it (Matt 16:18)! Sadly, it seems the rock couldn't stand the pressure and cracked before it could make it through that first tough night. Sad, indeed. What was to become of the church? Was this the end of the church before it even began? I'm sure the disciples couldn't help but wonder about their futures, too, especially Peter.

Thankfully, there's more to the story and yet another appearance of the number three. Fast-forward to the shore of the Sea of Galilee (John 21). It is after the resurrection, and several of the disciples went out and did the only thing they knew to do. They went fishing. After all, that's what they were doing when Jesus called them to be disciples in the first place. After a long night on the water, they returned to shore with empty nets and saw a man standing by a fire. He told them to cast their nets one more time on the other side of the boat, and they did. Their nets came up full. When they recognized that it was Jesus standing on the shore, Peter jumped out of the boat and waded on in. He was never any good at just sitting still. Jesus cooked them some breakfast and then took a stroll with Peter. While walking along the shore, Jesus asked Peter three times, "Do you love me?" Three times!

And each time Peter said that he did, and when he did, Jesus instructed him to tend to the flock and feed his sheep (John 21:15–17).

So, what does all of this have to do with sowing pardon where there is injury? Peter never came right out and apologized, and Jesus didn't come right out and say that he forgave him. Why? To begin, they didn't have to say anything. I think their body language told the story. Can you imagine the look on Peter's face? You could tell he was sorry, but he didn't know what to say. We've all been there. And Jesus sought Peter out. They shared a meal together before taking a stroll on the beach. Jesus' very presence spoke volumes through simple acts with an unforgettable message—you are forgiven. Hopefully, we've been there, too.

I think the fact that John tells us that Jesus asked Peter the same question three times, "Do you love me?" provides further insight. In addition to asking something three times to indicate just how serious the question was, and this question was serious, a triplet also meant that something was complete and good, like the trinity. So, asking Peter three times was not a scolding or an ugly reminder of his public failure. Rather, it was, as I read it, an act of enormous kindness. Jesus was communicating to Peter that he was complete and good just as he was right there on the beach. He was whole, and so was his mission to build the church. He wasn't on probation or damaged goods or required to appear before a committee to report what he had learned from his failure. He was the rock, good and complete. Not Simon, but Peter!

And I think there is good news here for all of us if we can find ourselves in this story, too. Clearly, we all come up short from time to time, just like Peter. We make brash promises, but we don't always deliver, and we are so very hard on ourselves when this happens. We feel like failures. However, Jesus doesn't see us as damaged goods or on probation or unreliable. In his eyes, we are all three-timers, good and complete, and so is our mission, our calling, and our ministry, whatever that happens to be. He asks us three times, "Do you love me?" We respond, "Lord, you know that I do!" "Ok then," he tells each of us, "let's get on with the work!"

## PRACTICING THE PRAYER OF ST. FRANCIS

This forgiving business can be complicated. In so many instances, it is hard to muster up the courage and humility to ask for forgiveness when we are the injuring party, even when we know that it is the right thing to do. It is hard to know how to walk with someone who has been injured, wanting to take charge or make it all go away, but such strategies seldom work. And if we are honest, it can be hard to forgive someone who has hurt us, and even harder to move on when we are in a situation where trust has been broken but the hope or necessity of an ongoing relationship remains. These are, all of them, difficult journeys.

When we pray to be an instrument of God's peace by sowing pardon where there is injury, something deeply spiritual is required of us that goes way beyond good intentions. We are called to practice *enormous kindness*. It is an enormous act of kindness when we gently accept an apology. It is an enormous act of kindness when we walk with someone who has been injured, respecting their dignity, hearing their anger, and honoring their own timetable for recovery without shifting the spotlight to ourselves. And it is an enormous act of kindness to forgive ourselves, especially when the voices in our heads keep telling us that we are unworthy and undesirable.

At the end of the day, it is the practice of kindness that makes forgiveness possible. It is a practice that summons something from deep within us, and it is sustained by a loving kindness that God has already extended to each of us. I do not believe that we can just say the Prayer of St. Francis and start being kind that very instant. It isn't some kind of magic trick. But we can be kinder each day, starting today, and as we focus on kindness, our prayers to sow pardon where there is injury will become a reality.

## A FINAL THOUGHT

The words of the prophet Joel are a fitting benediction: "Rend your heart and not your garments. Return to the Lord your God, for he is gracious and compassionate, slow to anger and abounding in love" (Joel 2:13). May we also be gracious and compassionate, slow to anger and abounding in love as we practice the Prayer of St. Francis, sowing pardon where there is injury.

## QUESTIONS FOR REFLECTION AND DISCUSSION

1. If you decided today to be kinder, where would you start? What three specific things could you do?

2. Is it harder for you to ask for forgiveness or to forgive others? Why?

3. Have you ever received an insincere apology? What did you do in that situation? What can you do in such instances?

4. What options would you have if you offered a sincere apology, but it was rebuffed or simply ignored? What would you do?

5. Would you agree that extending forgiveness is a spiritual act, even in the most mundane, everyday instances? How are we shaped by such small events?

The Prayer of St. Francis
*Lord, make me an instrument of your peace.*
*Where there is hatred, let me sow love;*
*Where there is injury, pardon;*

# 3

## Sowing Faith Where There Is Doubt

### *The Practice of Hospitality*

Immediately the boy's father exclaimed, "I do believe; help me overcome
my unbelief!"

—MARK 9:24

### INTRODUCTION

According to the Gospel of Mark (9), Peter, James, and John accompanied
Jesus to a high mountain. There, they witnessed the transfiguration. His
clothing became as white as snow, and Elijah and Moses appeared and talked
with Jesus. Then a cloud came and surrounded them, and a voice from the
cloud said: "This is my son, whom I love. Listen to him!" (Mark 9:7). As you
might expect, the disciples were both amazed and frightened. We would be,
too. They suggested building a string of monuments to commemorate the
strange event, but Jesus thought better of it. They tried to understand what
Jesus meant when he spoke of rising from the dead, but before too long, they
were arguing about who would be in charge if and when Jesus left the scene.
Apparently, the words from the cloud didn't sink in. They didn't listen.

Amid these events, a father came to Jesus and asked for healing for his son who was possessed by an impure spirit. Jesus responded, "'Everything is possible for one who believes.' Immediately the boy's father exclaimed, 'I do believe; help me overcome my unbelief!'" (Mark 9:23b–24). I believe that this is one of the most honest and humble responses ever recorded in Scripture. "Are you asking me if I believe? Of course, I do! I'm sure I do. After all, I traveled all day and fought through this crowd to bring my son to you. Surely, I believe, but help me overcome my unbelief. I have faith, but I have my doubts, too."

I think this earnest father speaks for all of us. Do we believe? Of course, we do! We know we do, at least most of the time. We have faith, but we have our doubts, too. In this chapter, we'll first examine the reality of doubt, and then discuss what it might mean for us to sow faith where there is doubt, especially when doubt lingers very close to home.

## Doubts

In my home church, the apostle Thomas was not a welcome guest. I can't recall a single sermon suggesting anything good about Thomas or the doubts he openly expressed. After all, he was known as Doubting Thomas, and that wasn't a positive nickname. It all started soon after the resurrection when Jesus appeared to the disciples, but Thomas was not there at the time. When he returned, the other disciples excitedly reported that Jesus had appeared to them, but Thomas said to them, "Unless I see the nail marks in his hands and put my finger where the nails were, and put my hand into his side, I will not believe" (John 20:25). Doubting Thomas, indeed.

His names, Thomas (in Aramaic) or Didymus (in Greek), mean the same thing—the twin, and I know a great deal about his twin. I am his twin, and if I am not mistaken, so are most of us. Most of us carry far more doubts than we will ever admit or even know, let alone face. After all, how can we have faith if we are doubters, too? Doesn't faith remove all our doubts? Well, yes and no. The answer is yes if you grew up or remain a part of a tradition that gives no credence to doubts. In my own tradition, doubts were seen as an indication of spiritual weakness. *Once Jesus comes into your life,* we were told, *all doubts are gone, and life is filled with joy and certainty.* Doubts were simply out, and even if you suspected that you might have a doubt or two, it would be better not to think about it—and certainly not share your doubts with anyone.

The answer is no, however, if you see doubts as an important part of the faith formation process. I remember going to the altar as a teenager and hearing the elders pray for me: "Hold on!" one would pray, while another prayed, "Let go!" I used to think that I was supposed to hold on to what little faith I had and let go of any doubts I might carry. The more I have reflected on those moments, however, I now believe that it is the other way around. I should hold on to my doubts and let go of a faith that demands a level of certainty that eliminates all questioning and any hope of spiritual growth. Doubts do not stunt our desire for spiritual formation, but blind certainty will every time. After all, why would we ask any questions if we already knew all the answers? The truth is we wouldn't, and in my view, that would be a shame.

The apostle Paul, one of the most ardent believers I can think of, wrote to the church in Corinth, "For now we see only a reflection as in a mirror; then we shall see face to face. Now I know in part; then I shall know fully, even as I am fully known" (1 Cor 13:12). Clearly, Paul didn't see and know everything, yet his faith persisted. In the same way, our faith can persist, too, not by pushing away or ignoring our doubts but by embracing them. As it turns out, doubts can be an ever-present friend. They keep us thinking, keep us asking questions, and keep us seeking the truth as they accompany us on our way home. At the end of the day, it is not a sin to acknowledge and share our doubts. Rather, it is an indication of a deep desire for spiritual growth. It is an act of faith.

Lord, we believe—help our unbelief.

## Sowing Faith Where There Is Doubt

I have been arguing that doubts are not contrary to faith. In fact, they are an ever-present friend if we desire to grow in our faith. I'm sure Abraham had his doubts when he obeyed and left his homeland for a new destination, "even though he did not know where he was going" (Heb 11:8b), and Sarah, his wife, surely had her doubts when she was told that she would bear a son despite being ninety years old (Gen 18:12). We know that Moses had his doubts about leading the children of Israel out of bondage, so much so that his older brother, Aaron, was assigned to accompany him as his spokesperson (Exod 4:13–16). Gideon tested the Lord with the fleece and then asked for a do-over—just to be sure (Judg 6:26–40). Jacob had his doubts about returning home, so he positioned his wives and children out in front as he went to meet his brother, Esau (Gen 33:2). And even John the Baptist had his doubts, sending two of his disciples to ask Jesus, "Are you the one who is to come, or should we expect someone else?" (Matt 11:3). I could name many others, but I think you get the point. Even the most faithful, including most of those who are highlighted in Heb 11 (known as the Faith Chapter in the Bible) had their doubts. It is simply part of the human condition, part of the life of faith.

So, how do we sow faith where there is doubt? First, we acknowledge our own doubts. We all have them, so let them see the light of day. They need not be hidden or ignored.

Second, we can embrace our doubts, appreciating them as a vital part of our spiritual formation process. They keep us questioning, keep us thinking, keep us moving, and keep us from getting stuck in the clutches of certainty that subtly demand that we check our minds at the door when we enter church or think about God or read the Bible.

Third, we can share our doubts with our discipleship group, with trusted friends, or with our pastor or spiritual advisor. God can take our doubts, and hopefully those who deeply care about us can as well. I once hesitantly shared with a New Testament scholar and close friend I admired that I didn't have the resurrection all figured out. In fact, I had some serious questions about what transpired that weekend and what it all means for my faith. He smiled and shared that he felt much the same way. I can't tell you what a relief it was to know that a deeply committed, serious minded Christian had doubts, too. I thought that I was the only one who did.

Finally, we can give safe space for others to express their doubts, too, and when they do, we embrace their questions and consider them holy, an honest and productive aspect of the faith-formation process. When we desire to sow faith where there is doubt, we begin by honestly acknowledging, embracing, and sharing our own while giving safe space, holy space, for others to do the same. And when we do, it provides fertile ground for a deeper faith to take root. Ultimately, I believe that we don't come to faith as much as faith comes to us. It is more about living faithfully than about believing earnestly.

## SCRIPTURE

"For I am convinced that neither death nor life, neither angels nor demons, neither the present nor the future, nor any powers, neither height nor depth, nor anything else in all creation, will be able to separate us from the love of God that is in Christ Jesus our Lord" (Rom 8:38–39). These words, penned by the apostle Paul for the church in Rome, speak for themselves and still speak to us today. If Paul is right, and I believe he is, then nothing in all creation can separate us from the love of God—*nothing*. In my view, that includes our doubts and questions, too—all of them. Thanks be to God.

## PRACTICING THE PRAYER OF ST. FRANCIS

Let me suggest three ways we can practice the Prayer of St. Francis as we seek to sow faith where there is doubt.

### Join the Conversation

Far too often, we think we are the only ones who have ever doubted a certain theological assertion or questioned some of the beliefs and practices of our local community of faith, and when we operate on that assumption, we tend to flounder in isolation or simply bury our doubts and smile as we leave church each week. The reality is this: you are rarely, if ever, dealing with questions that are entirely new. It is much more likely that you are just the most recent person to raise the question, not the first to do so. You are simply joining a sacred conversation, and these conversations have been going on for a very long time, centuries even.

So, join the conversation! Read and study about what concerns you. If you are concerned about atonement theory, for example, learn about it. See what others have written or said about these matters, especially those who may hold a different point of view. You certainly do not have to agree with or believe everything you read or hear, but the pursuit of truth is an eternal conversation about things that matter to you and to others. Just be sure to consider the source—everyone comes with certain assumptions in mind or a particular point of view to promote. That's ok, we do, too.

A good way to join the conversation is to enroll in a course offered at a nearby university or online. There are literally hundreds of courses on the Gospels or Paul's writings alone. Jump in, listen, learn, push back, read, and enjoy. It can be a life-giving experience, and as you will learn from any legitimate course and wise professor, good scholars disagree about a lot of things. Those who have given their entire adult lives to the consideration of these questions don't come out at the same place. If you don't learn anything else, it is good to come to the realization that the questions are far more interesting and energizing than a perfect answer that settles the question forever. Honestly, such answers don't exist. So, learn to hold questions in tension and enjoy the conversation, a meal best served with humility, good will, patience, and grace.

## Create Safe Spaces

Offering hospitality is one of the most formative spiritual practices I know, and it is fun, too! There is something sacred going on when we break bread together, and the dinner table can be a safe place where doubts are shared and compelling, even controversial, questions and concerns are discussed. Start by sharing your own. I have found that when I am open about what I have on my mind, it models that my table is a safe place for honest conversations. You can't expect others to share their hearts and minds with you unless they feel safe to do so. They will follow your lead.

And I have also found that several well-placed questions are far more inducive to deep conversations than any speech or sermon I might deliver, no matter how eloquent I am at the time. Creating safe spaces and helping others give voice to their doubts are truly acts of faith, faith in the Spirit of Truth, the ever-present teacher who guides us into all the truth (John 16:13).

## Find a Holy Place

It is important to have your own holy place, a sacred place where you return time and again for reading, writing, reflection, and prayer. It is a place where you can listen and contemplate as well as pour out your doubts and share your honest concerns and questions. I know it sounds a bit mystical, and in some ways it is, but we all need a space that we recognize as a holy place, a spiritual place, a sacred space—a place where we are honest and open before God and with God.

I am suggesting, no urging, all of us to find or create our own sacred places and use them regularly, not somewhere in Hawaii or among the Redwoods or along the Pacific coast, but right where we live and work—a place where we can return each day. And I have found it helpful to light a candle, play some music, or dim the lights—to do something tangible that signals that I am doing something holy, seeking the Holy One. It brings notice and focus to the time spent there. It is so easy to lose sight of the holy in our everyday activities, even though deep down we know that it is all holy. If we want to sow faith where there is doubt, the work starts at home in our own holy spaces.

## A FINAL THOUGHT

I am aware that this chapter may be confusing or downright disturbing to some of us, particularly if we come from a tradition where holding a certain set of theological beliefs is expected from everyone as an essential demonstration of the Christian faith, or from a tradition where faith is demonstrated by a certain set of required practices or behaviors that must be followed while others must be strictly avoided. In such traditions, expressing doubts is understood and treated as a lack of faith, leaving many of us to say to ourselves or a very close friend at one time or another, "If they really knew what I thought or believed about _____ [you put in the topic], they would be shocked and stop talking to me or run me out of this place." I've thought it many times myself.

I have tried to say in this chapter that our doubts are as important as our beliefs. They give shape and season to our faith. In my view, it is the demand for absolute certainty and compliance that restricts and suffocates the development of our faith as we all make our way home. So, my advice is to embrace your journey of faith, even if you don't know where you are going, avoid the swamp of certainty, stay on solid ground, and enjoy the adventure. Living faithfully is a trip of a lifetime.

For me, it all comes down to this: *Life is messy, but God is faithful.* That we can count on with certainly.

## QUESTIONS FOR REFLECTION AND DISCUSSION

1. Who are your role models for how to live a life of faith? What have they taught you?

2. Do you agree that doubts are helpful, even essential to faith formation? Explain.

3. Do you have a safe place to share your questions and doubts? If so, what makes it so, and if not, how might you create one for yourself and others?

4. Do you have a sacred space, a holy place, where you can return day after day? If not, how might you create one?

5. If you were to express that which you are most certain about in your faith journey in one sentence, what would it be?

The Prayer of St. Francis
*Lord, make me an instrument of your peace.*
*Where there is hatred, let me sow love;*
*Where there is injury, pardon;*
*Where there is doubt, faith;*

# 4

## Sowing Hope Where There Is Despair

### *The Practice of Courage*

We must accept finite disappointment, but never lose infinite hope.
—MARTIN LUTHER KING JR.

## INTRODUCTION

Elijah was at the top of his spiritual game. When we see him, he has just won a major public challenge to a "call-down-the-fire" contest against the prophets of Baal and Asherah, all 450 of them. They prayed and pleaded with their gods to no avail. Then, Elijah, in total control of the situation, taunted them and asked for water to be poured on the altar to make the feat even more remarkable, not seeming to remember how precious water was since the land was in the middle of a terrible drought, a drought he had predicted. No matter. After he won the contest and dispatched of the competition, the rains came. He was the ultimate victor, recognized by all as the servant of the true God (1 Kgs 18:16–45).

So, given all of this, why do we find Elijah, the champion, the winner, the victorious servant of God, sitting under a broom bush a day's journey into the wilderness, afraid for his life and wishing he could die (1 Kgs 19:3–5)?

True, Queen Jezebel had angrily threatened him, but why would despair creep in immediately following such a great spiritual victory? Did he forget God's faithfulness to him over the years? Did he forget being fed by ravens in the desert (1 Kgs 17:2–6)? Did he forget having a never-ending supply of flour and oil at the widow's house (1 Kgs 17:15–16), or God bringing her son back from the dead (1 Kgs 17:17–24)? And how could he forget that God, just the day before, demonstrated his might by crushing the prophets of Baal and Asherah and replenishing the drought-stricken land with rain?

Good questions, indeed. I think great successes can cause spiritual amnesia. It seems the wilderness is only a day's journey away for any of us. We either forget the faithfulness of God or we are dizzied and distracted by our accomplishments, or both, but even big successes can somehow leave us feeling terribly inadequate and very much alone. We often associate despair with failure, frustration, fatigue, and injury—times when the roof caves in, which it is, but being at the top of our spiritual game does not exempt us from these feelings either. Despair, it seems, is an equal opportunity offender.

So, how do we sow hope where there is despair? That is the major question we will address in this chapter. First, we'll look a bit more at despair and why it troubles our spirits so deeply before turning to the subject of hope, something we all can embrace. Then, we'll pick up the story of Elijah once more. I believe that it is a textbook example for how to sow hope in the wilderness of despair. Before closing, I will offer a few practical steps we can take when we despair or walk with those who do, choosing to find and sow hope rather than sitting under a broom bush and wishing to call it quits.

## Despair

Let's face it. Despair is tough; it is a serious matter. It can debilitate us both mentally and spiritually. When we feel that we have no options to change our circumstances, it can drain the life out of life. But hope, I will argue, is the great motivator. I believe that faith sends all of us on a spiritual journey and love bids us home, but it is hope that keep us going in good times and bad. And, fortunately for all of us, it is a renewable resource.

Despair is a feeling of helplessness, realizing that something is profoundly wrong and there is nothing we can do to make it go away or make life better. Circumstances are simply beyond our control, too much for us to manage or change. We feel that we have no choices, so we trudge through each day without any sense of meaning, joy, or hope. Each day is miserable, and there is no end of the misery in sight.

Just look at some of the words that are associated with despair: gloom, melancholy, pain, desperation, sorrow, despondency, discouragement, anguish, ordeal, dejection, trial, tribulation, wretchedness, forlornness, and disheartenment. You can easily sense the misery in these words. Living without hope or feeling that a situation is hopeless kills the spirit. We end each day not anticipating a better tomorrow. In fact, the dread is that all our tomorrows will be just like today—pure misery.

And despair can come upon us at unexpected times and in unexpected ways. It might be a word from the doctor, an accident, the loss of a job or relationship, an embarrassment, or a phone call in the middle of the night. One day we are taunting the prophets of Baal and Asherah, and the next day we find ourselves sitting under a broom bush wishing that it was all over. In fact, feeling that it *is* all over.

One thing is for certain. This is not a pull-yourself-up-by-your-own-bootstraps kind of moment, and there are no easy answers or quick fixes. No "when life gives you lemons, make lemonade" or "when God closes a door, a window will be left open" bromides to perk up your spirit and brighten up your day. When in despair, what we need most seems in short supply, totally out of reach—hope. So, how might we walk with someone who so desperately needs to find some hope in the circumstances they face? Is it even possible to sow hope where there is despair? Admittedly, it can be a daunting task, but I believe that there is much to be learned about sowing a sense of hope and purpose from the story of Elijah, but first let's be clear about what we mean when we speak of hope.

## Hoping

Hope can be a verb, something we do, akin to wishing. When I was twelve, I received a weather station from my parents as a Christmas present, capable of measuring temperature, wind speed, barometric pressure, and humidity (well, sort of). I had dreams of becoming a weatherman, working for a local TV station in Saginaw, but that all changed when my least favorite uncle arrived for Christmas dinner. He took joy in unkindly teasing and embarrassing his nephews, and this occasion was no exception. In a loud voice in front of the entire extended family (about twenty-five in total), he demanded a prediction: "Since you are so smart now with your new weather station, when will it snow? We want a prediction."

I don't think he knew how shy I was or how much I hated to be embarrassed—just hated it! All eyes were on me, and I felt my face getting red.

Honestly, I didn't know what to do, but from somewhere deep inside these words spilled out: "It will snow by four o'clock today."

"Really?" my uncle retorted. "We'll see how good of a weatherman you are."

That last statement ruined my entire day. From eleven o'clock on, my uncle called out each half hour, "Is it snowing yet?" with a not-so-nice grin.

"Not yet," I would say, looking to the west, hoping for any sign of snow. There was none—mostly clear skies. The waiting was terribly painful, and the closer it got to four o'clock, the worse I felt. This was certainly not the Christmas I had anticipated.

Honestly, I nearly lost all hope. Then a miracle happened. Just a minute or two before four o'clock, some tiny snowflakes came drifting down, looking more like ashes from a campfire than snow flurries. It wasn't much, and it didn't last very long, but I declared it to be a snowfall and my family didn't protest. As we sat down for Christmas dinner, somehow my spirit was renewed. Christmas had been saved.

I learned a few lessons that day. To begin with, hoping and waiting are really hard. They test your spirit, especially so when the stakes are high— like hoping the latest lab tests bring good news, waiting for the phone to ring after a job interview, or praying for someone to make it home during a bad storm, and for a shy, fragile, tender young boy, for it to start snowing before four o'clock on Christmas Day. Hoping isn't always easy, but I have come to believe that it is an honest act of faith, a prayer for what we do not yet see. And it can be a spiritual practice, too, shaping us in ways known and unknown.

I learned that we sometimes put ourselves unnecessarily in situations where hope is fading and despair is pulling in the driveway. On that Christmas day, there were several ways that I could have avoided having the weather determine my Christmas experience, something totally out of my control. For example, I could have brushed off my uncle's demand for a prediction, stating that the station was not yet functioning or that I needed several days of data to make a prediction. I could have made it clear that it wasn't possible to precisely state when a storm would arrive without radar, or I could have just laughed at his comment and returned one of my own: "Ha! That's funny. Maybe next year!" Of course, these are adult responses, and I was a child. However, I wonder how many times we find ourselves hoping beyond hope in situations we could have avoided with a little wisdom and forethought. I think it is always a fair question to ask when we begin to despair and lose hope—what is it that we are hoping for? Could it be that we set ourselves up for despair by depending on circumstances that no one can influence or control?

And I learned to believe in miracles. Now I realize that predicting snow in Central Michigan in late December is not really going out on much of a limb, but the skies were mostly clear that day. Of course, it could have been just a lucky coincidence. I grant you that. But then again, could it be that the God of the universe saw a little boy losing hope and praying for snow in the face of ridicule, embarrassment, and shame, and decided to send just a few tiny snowflakes his way? I honestly believe that that's what happened. Albert Einstein is quoted as saying that you either believe that nothing is a miracle or that everything is.[1] I tend to go with the latter. To this very day, I smile every time I see falling snow, acknowledging all the snowflakes in my life—the remembered and forgotten signs of hope, the manifestations of God's love and grace.[2]

## Hope

Hope can also be a noun, something we carry with us, the feeling of expectation or desire for a certain thing to happen. The expectation that something will happen implies more of a sense of certainty or confidence, while the desire for a certain outcome seems a bit more like wishing, but they are both manifestations of hope, the fuel that keeps us going in tough and terrible times, and good times, too. However, hope can be placed in many things—in our gifts and graces, our popularity, our contacts, our resources, our education, our jobs, our families, even our churches, and despair comes quickly into play when these places let us down, and at one time or another, they all will.

So where can we place our hope? "Those who hope in the Lord will renew their strength. They will soar on wings like eagles; they will run and not grow weary, they will walk and not faint," the prophet Isaiah tells us (Isa 40:31). I think he's right. And the apostle Paul writes this about hope, "May the God of hope fill you with all joy and peace as you trust in him, so that you may overflow with hope by the power of the Holy Spirit" (Rom 15:13). I like that very much, too—the God of hope brings joy and peace as you trust in him, and hope overflows by the power of the Holy Spirit. So, where can we place our hope? We can place our hope in the character and promises of God.

All of this begs two essential questions: what *are* we hoping for, and where *do* we place our hope? Our answers will reveal much about our ability

1. Einstein, "There Are Only Two Ways."

2. Some of this reflection about hoping for snow first appeared in Allen, *Love at Its Best*, 144–45. Used by permission.

to sow hope where there is despair, especially in our own lives. Let's look at how God planted seeds of hope with Elijah and then turn our attention to how we might sow seeds of hope as we put the Prayer of St. Francis into practice each day in our own neighborhoods.

## SCRIPTURE

We pick up the story of Elijah, the famous prophet, sitting under a broom bush in deep despair and asking the Lord to take his life (1 Kgs 19). He takes a nap but is awoken by an angel who brings him fresh bread and a jar of water—twice, and both times urges him to get up and eat. The second time Elijah is told that he needed to set out on a long journey to Mount Horeb, a pilgrimage of sorts, and there God would meet him. When he reaches Mount Horeb, he spends the night in a cave (vv. 5–9).

The Lord asks Elijah: "What are you doing here?" (1 Kgs 19:10). Elijah reports that although he has been very zealous for the Lord God Almighty, he is now the only faithful one left. God speaks to Elijah, but not in a great and powerful wind, not in a mighty earthquake, and not in a roaring fire. Rather, in a gentle whisper the Lord asks Elijah again: "What are you doing here?" Elijah repeats his answer—he has been zealous for the Lord but is now the only one left. The Lord instructs Elijah to go back the way he came and go to the Desert of Damascus, where he was to anoint Hazel as king over Aram, Jehu, a king over Israel, and Elisha as the prophet to take his place. This trio would take care of all who worshiped Baal. And incidentally, the Lord mentions to Elijah in passing that there are "seven thousand in Israel—all whose knees have not bowed down to Baal and whose mouths have not kissed him" (1 Kgs 19:18). Obviously, Elijah wasn't the only faithful one left. It only felt that way.

## PRACTICING THE PRAYER OF ST. FRANCIS

Elijah's story is truly amazing, full of wisdom for all of us who pray to sow hope where there is despair. I want to highlight six insights from the story and discuss how we might learn to practice what we pray by offering fresh bread, embracing a long journey, asking honest questions, letting God be God, challenging false assumptions, and accepting a new mission—practices that can lead to hope and spiritual renewal.

## Offer Fresh Bread

As Elijah curled up under a broom bush in deep despair, an angel brought a loaf of fresh bread. For me, this is a metaphor for offering spiritual comfort and nourishment to someone in need. I don't know about you, but when I am on my own, alone, weekends are the hardest. I guess that during the week, there are enough activities, appointments, lunches, meetings, and projects to keep my mind occupied and my heart distracted, but everything slows down on the weekend. Uninvited thoughts and feelings creep in, and the nights can be very, very lonely. I experienced this phenomenon full force while working in San Diego. Going through a divorce, even under the best of conditions, if there is such a thing as the best of conditions, is painful to say the least, and particularly so in a conservative Christian community. Honestly, my constant companions were guilt, shame, and fear—uninvited companions who whispered in the dark of the night, *You are not worthy, you are not trustworthy, and you are no longer welcome in this place.* I thought that I would lose my job and there was nothing that I could do about it. I carried and nurtured these feelings like a newborn baby. I was in despair.

Then out of the blue, three friends stepped forward and each volunteered to be my companion—committed to helping me make it through the long and lonely weekends ahead. I don't think they colluded, but each one took a specific block of the weekend. The first companion simply wouldn't let me attend church on my own. When you are suffering and down for any reason, attending church on your own is very difficult. On several occasions, I would come to the side entrance of the sanctuary, look in, and simply turn around and go home. At other times, I would slip in and sit by myself, and make a hasty exit as soon as the benediction was pronounced. That was even worse. However, my friend would not let me stay away. He insisted that I come to church, sit with his family, and then come over for Sunday lunch before joining the family in some rousing table games. From time to time, I would purposely cheat just a bit, doing so obviously so that his children would see what I was doing. They loved to catch me and call out my transgressions. We would all have a big laugh as I promised to learn all the rules. I don't think I ever won even a game, but I was the true winner. To this day, I have fond memories of those Sunday afternoons when I was offered a loaf of fresh bread—literally and spiritually.

The second friend took the Friday night shift. Even though he was working two jobs and had teenage children, he told me that he was committed to spending each Friday evening with me over the fall semester. I immediately protested, pointing out that he had a family of his own, but he wouldn't take no for an answer. He told me that he had already talked it over with his wife and family, and they all thought that this was a good thing to do. So, every Friday evening that fall we met for dinner, then went to a movie or a hockey game or just drank coffee and talked theology and church politics. And as we did, he walked with me and watched over me, offering me another loaf of fresh bread each week.

My third friend became my Saturday companion, or more precisely, I became his shadow. Sometimes we would hike or attend a sporting event, or go to Home Depot, or just hang out at home with his family. I became quite good at helping mow the fields, trim the trees, and even repair a fence post or two. I simply joined in with whatever his family was doing that day, and it was life-giving. He would always ask me how I was doing. On one occasion, I admitted that I was having trouble going through each day being sure that I didn't act *too* happy. After all, I was damaged goods, and I was told that I shouldn't be joyful. I should just be thankful that I still had a job, at least for the time being. He stared at me for a minute, then cleared his throat and asked, "Has anyone given you permission to look to the future with some anticipation, even joy?" Of course, my answer was no. "Well, I do!" he barked as he gave me an even longer and more intense stare. I received that loaf of bread full force. As I look back, that was the turning point for me. I started to look ahead, albeit self-consciously, to better days, and in due time they did come.

Clearly, these three friends held my hand and walked next to me. In one of the darkest times I have ever known, they were with me, affirming their hopes and dreams for me even when I didn't have any of my own. They offered fresh bread, and it sustained me. There isn't a day that goes by when I don't think of their care for me, and I pray for opportunities to share a loaf of bread—literally and spiritually—with other suffering souls. As it turns out, they are everywhere.[3]

## Embrace the Journey

When we are walking with someone in despair or dealing with our own, it is important to understand that the healing process is a long journey, not a quick fix—a marathon, not a sprint. Notice that the angel didn't send Elijah back to the place of his last victory, although it was only a day's walk away. Instead, he was told that he needed strength for a long journey. According to 1 Kgs 19:8, Elijah was to travel forty days and forty nights to Mt. Horeb, the mountain of God. As we noted in chapter 2, the number forty can literally

---

3. A previous version of this story first appeared in Allen, *Good Shepherd*, 111–13. Used by permission.

mean forty, but it usually means a very long time, a period of new life, new growth, a transition from one great task to another. I think it fair to understand Elijah's journey of forty days and forty nights as a transition from one great task to another, one that would take some time to process and embrace.

This is a good reminder for all of us when we deal with feelings of despair. The recovery process is a marathon, not a sprint. The approach to training and the strategy to complete these races are totally different. If we enter a marathon thinking that it is like a sprint, just longer, we won't make it through the first five miles. Much the same can be said when dealing with despair. If we think there's some kind of quick fix or presto moment when despair simply and quickly goes away like a mild headache, we are traveling on the well-worn wishing road. The right road stretches out before us, a journey to be embraced, requiring a long-view perspective, patience, persistence, and courage.

## Ask Honest Questions

A third way to practice the prayer of St. Francis when we desire to sow hope where there is despair is to ask honest questions. The temptation, of course, is to provide answers and sayings instead of asking questions. It is not helpful to inform someone in despair that your aunt experienced much the same thing and then go on to tell them in great detail just how she dealt with it, or to tell someone that all they need to do is pray harder and read the Bible more. And offering such encouragements as "it could be worse" or "diamonds are formed under conditions of intense heat and pressure" are not encouraging at all, no matter how well intended. I even heard a radio host exclaim this encouragement: "When God shuts a door, he will leave a window open—or at least keep the doggie-door unlocked!" In my view, such statements invite more despair, not less.

The key, I believe, is to practice holy silence as best you can, and if you do speak, ask honest questions about how despair is being experienced instead of dispensing uninvited and unwelcome advice. God asked Elijah, "What you are doing here?" Elijah's answer provides a clue to his despair: "I have been very zealous for the Lord God Almighty. The Israelites have rejected your covenant, torn down your altars, and put your prophets to death with the sword. I am the only one left, and now they are trying to kill me too" (1 Kgs 19:10). Here, for the first time, Elijah puts his fears and disappointments into words—"I have been zealous, but the Israelites have rejected your covenant. I am the only one left who has not abandoned you,

Lord. And by the way, where were you when I needed you and why haven't you come in a mighty way to rescue me? I don't want to die!!"

This is a good start. Elijah begins to put into words how he is feeling and what he believes is going on, even if he is a bit mistaken about some of it. When we ask honest questions, we are letting others give voice to their despair, to lament, and in doing so, we are putting our prayers into practice.

## Let God Be God

Elijah was a zealot of sorts, a firebrand, and that was his understanding of God, too, so when he journeyed to Mt. Horeb, he looked for God in the mighty wind, then in a massive earthquake, and finally in a raging fire, but God was not there. Rather, God came and spoke to Elijah in a gentle whisper. He almost missed hearing from God because he was looking and listening for a big display of power and might, the way he perceived God to be. It is a formative spiritual practice to let God be God, to look for his work and listen for his voice all the time, in places you expect God to be, and especially in places where you don't expect him to be, and let God speak in a gentle whisper even though we would rather see a firestorm. When we are in despair or walking with those who are, it is easy to limit God by our own preconceived notions about how God works and what we want to see happen. To practice the Prayer of St. Francis, we let God be God and listen for his voice as an act of faith, seeds sown in hope.

## Challenge False Assumptions

Earlier I suggested that when we ask honest questions, we are letting others give voice to their despair, to lament, and in doing so, we are putting our prayers into practice. I truly believe that to be true. We ask honest questions, and we listen as despair is put into words, even our own words. But just because we think or feel a certain way doesn't make it true. There will be times when we will need to lean in gently and challenge the facts of the lament we hear. And if we are dealing with our own despair, the honest questions and a reality check from a trusted friend or advisor can be hope-giving.

Elijah firmly believed that he was the only faithful one left in Israel. I'm sure he felt that way, but it just wasn't true. God reminded him that there were seven thousand in Israel who did not bow to Baal (1 Kgs 19:18). This news was important for at least two reasons. First, in large part, his despair was because he thought he was the only faithful one left in all the land and that he had to fight the battles all by himself. Of course, this was not true.

And second, God wanted to give Elijah a new mission, a mantle that would be unrealistic to even consider if he thought he was all alone. When we challenge false assumptions or our own false assumptions are challenged, it clears the way to consider what God may have in store for us, things full of challenge and hope.

## Accept a New Mission

After Elijah understood that he was not the only one left, in fact, there were seven thousand eager to fight, he was probably ready to return as the zealous prophet and lead them into battle, but God had a different mission for him. He was to go back and anoint Hazel king of Aram, Jehu king of Israel, and Elisha as his own successor as prophet. He was to pass the torch to the next generation of leaders. I doubt that this was what Elijah expected or necessarily wanted, but after taking spiritual bread, embracing his journey, giving expression to his despair, hearing God in a new way, and seeing that he was not alone, he was willing to believe that God had something different for him to do. In fact, he was the only one for this new mission. Out of despair comes the possibility of a renewed faith in God and a hope for the future.

## A FINAL THOUGHT

There is much that we can glean from the story of Elijah as we deal with our own despair or walk with those who do, but one question remains. Did Elijah find hope or did he remain in despair? We are told that Elijah did as God requested and went back to work. He anointed the trio and the battle against the prophets of Baal was on, and Elijah began grooming Elisha as his successor. When it was clear that Elijah was about to die, he asked Elisha, "Tell me, what can I do for you before I am taken from you?" Elisha replied, "Let me inherit a double portion of your spirit" (2 Kgs 2:9). A double portion of his spirit, indeed. Clearly, his spirit was back.

The last obligation of a leader is to make a graceful exit, to look to the next generation, and to pass on wisdom, spirit, and hope. Well done, Elijah.

## QUESTIONS FOR REFLECTION AND DISCUSSION

1. On a personal and a spiritual level, what are you hoping for?
2. Who is the most hopeful person you know? Why so?

3. At a low point in your life, who offered you a loaf of bread? Explain.

4. Has God ever spoken to you in an unexpected way? How so?

5. Can you point to a leader who made a graceful exit, passing the torch to the next generation of leaders? What personal and spiritual qualities made a smooth transition possible?

The Prayer of St. Francis
*Lord, make me an instrument of your peace.*
*Where there is hatred, let me sow love;*
*Where there is injury, pardon;*
*Where there is doubt, faith;*
*Where there is despair, hope;*

# 5

# Sowing Light Where There Is Darkness

## *The Practice of Guidance*

We can easily forgive a child who is afraid of the dark;

the real tragedy of life is when men are afraid of the light.

—PLATO

## INTRODUCTION

The Gospel of John tells us that some Greeks came to celebrate the Passover in Jerusalem, and they approached Phillip, one of Jesus' disciples, with a request. They wanted to see Jesus (John 12:20–21). It wasn't clear what they meant by "seeing" Jesus. Did they want to see Jesus perform a miracle to demonstrate his awesome power or produce some signs and wonders? Did they want to see a healing, or perhaps be healed themselves? Did they want to hear him preach or teach from the law? Did they want to question him, or possibly get a selfie, standing arm in arm with him and smiling like Cheshire cats, to send back to their friends in Athens? Certainly, there is no indication that they wanted to follow him. They simply said that they wanted to see Jesus, and we don't exactly know what they meant.

In many ways, the same can be said about the word *light*. We don't always know exactly what it means when we hear it. It is a common word, used in Scripture well over two hundred times. Sometimes it is used literally, as in "And God said, 'Let there be light,' and there was light. God saw that the light was good, and he separated the light from the darkness" (Gen 1:3–4), or "No one lights a lamp and hides it in a clay jar or puts it under a bed. Instead, they put it on a stand, so that those who come in can see the light" (Luke 8:16). More times than not, however, light is used as a spiritual metaphor or a part of a larger teaching metaphor: "When Jesus spoke again to the people, he said, 'I am the light of the world. Whoever follows me will never walk in darkness, but will have the light of life'" (John 8:12). On another occasion, Jesus said, "I have come into the world as a light, so that no one who believes in me should stay in darkness" (John 12:46). And the apostle Paul put even more emphasis on light when he wrote to the church in Ephesus, "For you were once darkness, but now you are light in the Lord. Live as children of light" (Eph 5:8). Clearly, light can mean different things to different people on different occasions, but the implications are clear. We are to be children of light—sowing light, not darkness.

So, when we pray, asking God to help us sow light where there is darkness, what exactly are we praying for? What are we intending to do, and how do we go about doing so? What light are we talking about? In some ways, we've been sowing light where there is darkness from the beginning of this prayer. We have addressed the darkness of hatred, injury, doubt, and despair—really dark things. And we have prayed to sow love, pardon, faith, and hope—ways to let the light of the Holy Spirit shine in and through us. Yet after all these good things, St. Francis writes, "Where there is darkness, [let me sow] light." I guess he felt that there was still some sowing to do, and who can argue with the author, a saint.

In most metaphors in Scripture, light has to do in some way or another with spiritual illumination—with finding our way, coming to know the truth, or living in a way that pleases God (living a well-ordered life). In this chapter, we will take the confession and testimony of Jesus seriously, "I am the light of the world. Whoever follows me will not walk in darkness . . ." (John 8:12). Jesus also told his disciples that he was the way and the truth and the life (John 14:6). Of course, on one level, this is a spiritual metaphor—a mystery, but on another level, it is a helpful way to frame our consideration of light, and how we might sow light where there is darkness. As it turns out, light is necessary to find our way, to know the truth, and to live a life pleasing to God. No one can do these things in the dark. They require light.

Honestly, sowing light is a daunting task and an audacious prayer. John encourages us, "But if we walk in the light, as he is in the light, we have fellowship with one another, and the blood of Jesus, his Son, purifies us from all sin" (1 John 1:7). Let's start walking!

## Finding the Way

Wouldn't it be nice if we had a built-in GPS system that would keep us on the right path, and if we wandered off the path, it would simply announce, "Recalculating, recalculating," and then new directions would be given without condemnation, anger, or frustration; just a simple course correction as we made our way home? It certainly would be nice, especially when we lose our way in the dark—or we're stuck in a dark place. We are frozen in place, staring and listening in the darkness, hoping for a sign, any sign, that might help us know which way to go. Traveling in the dark can be disorienting, frightening, and dangerous, too. Let me mention three ways that we can sow light in the darkness, helping those who have lost their way, and that is most of us at one time or another.

### Fence Posts

If you have ever had the pleasure of walking or hunting in a deciduous forest just after the leaves fall and before the snow flies, you know that the wire fences running through the woods are almost invisible, but not so the fence posts. Most metal ones have a painted white top, and they are easily spotted since the white color seems out of place in the middle of the brown and grey underbrush. They quickly catch your eye. Those white tops have saved me more than once from walking full steam into a fence row while hunting. They served as an early warning system of sorts, signaling to me to take care and watch where I was going. All was not as it appeared to be at first glance.

And fence posts also support the fence that marks out a plot of land or territory. A study of school children playing next to a busy street found that they used only about 60 percent of the playground. As you might expect, they were constantly being warned to "stay out of the street" and "don't play near the road." They did their best of keep the rules, but it was difficult, especially when a ball rolled into the middle of the street or they tried to avoid being "it" during a game of tag. The school decided to fence in the playground. Now the children could play right next to the fence without fear, and they could even use the fence as a backstop in some of their games. As a result, 100 percent of the playground was used as intended. The fence provided protection, a safe perimeter, and a boundary that marked out safe territory.

I think that all of us need spiritual fences and fence posts as we strive to find our way, especially in the darkness. We need lights that shine on the boundaries to let us know where it is safe to go and when we need to take caution. We all know of good people who "crossed the line" of one kind or another, and they (and their families) paid a huge price. They didn't notice the fence posts, crossed into unhealthy territory, and ended up in a very dark, deep thicket of their own doing.

In the darkness, we all need light in the form of accountability—friends, the wisdom of Scripture, a small group, our own experience, or that still small voice that calls us out and calls to us to pay attention. We need a light to shine on our doings and desires, to spotlight when we are headed for the underbrush at full speed in the dark, even when we don't want to admit that we are and we tell others that we know exactly what we are doing. A light shining on a friend's path or on our own is a form of grace, guiding when we have lost our sense of true north, helping to illuminate what dangers await when we stray off the path or deliberately choose to go our own way.

If we want to sow light where there is darkness, we can be fence posts.

## Guideposts

While fence posts create a boundary for safe travel and correction when headed off the path, guideposts let us know that we are on the right path and show us the way to go from here. Some guideposts even tell us how much farther it is to the next fork in the road, always a decision point. When we are hiking on a new path in unfamiliar surroundings, a guidepost is such a welcome sight. It says in effect, "Welcome, you're doing fine; you're on the right path; keep going; here's the way." When you come to a guidepost on the trail, there is reassurance and a deep sense of relief, knowing that someone has been here before you, wherever "here" is, and you can make your way, too. Someone has marked the way for you.

And this is particularly true when it starts to get dark. It is so easy to get lost in the dark when you can't see more than a few feet in front of you. There is no horizon to provide perspective, direction, or a long view. In such cases, a guidepost can be the difference between finding your way home and totally losing your way.

When I think of spiritual guideposts, I think of role models—individuals in my life who have been where I want to go, who demonstrate how to live faithfully in this world and how to prepare for the journey to the next with confidence, courage, contentment, and grace. When we pray to sow light where there is darkness, we are volunteering to let our lights shine, too—to be role models for someone in a dark place. Thankfully, a little bit of light can dispel a great deal of darkness. We are not required to be superheroes or saints, just plain, honest folk who love Jesus and who are willing to walk with our neighbors, pointing the way as best we can.

If we want to sow light where there is darkness, we can be guideposts.

### Lampposts

One final post bears mentioning—a lamppost. There is nothing more comforting to a traveler than to see that the lights are on and someone is home. Coming out of the woods after dark or making your way through a terrible storm, just the glimpse of a lamppost warms the heart. You know you're almost home. Sometimes in the middle of a very dark time or place, it is the only thing that keeps you going.

There are spiritual lampposts all around us that point the way home. There are the testimonies of those who have traveled the road we are on, a veritable cloud of witnesses. There are friends, family, mentors, and role models who walk with us and encourage us even as they point the way forward. Moreover, there are the many promises found in Scripture, such as the words of Jesus: "I am going there to prepare a place for you" (John 14:2b), and there is that still small voice of the Holy Spirit who speaks to us in the middle of our darkness: "I am with you, I will guide you, follow my voice." Let's look and be thankful for the lampposts in our own lives, even as we strive to keep the lights on for those around us.

If we want to sow light where there is darkness, we can be a lampposts.[1]

## Knowing the Truth

We can not only lose our way in the dark, but we can also be literally in the dark. That is, we don't have a clue about what is going on. Have you ever walked into a room where everyone else seems to have been told what was about to happen next—maybe a surprise party or an unexpected recognition—but you didn't have a clue? Others will say later with great joy, "We kept you in the dark on this one, and you didn't see it coming!" Of course, dealing with this kind of darkness, not knowing, is not harmful. In fact, it

---

1. A discussion of posts first appeared in Allen, *Good Shepherd*, 129–31.

can make the celebration richer, even if it comes with a small dose of embar-rassment on your part. My mother was fond of saying that eating humble pie in small doses can be good for you. I think she was right.

But we can also find ourselves in the dark, unable to see clearly that which is right in front of us. We cautiously stumble along with our arms outstretched, hoping to feel the wall before we run into it or stub a toe on a chair leg. That's not a bad mode of travel if we're trying to make our way across a dark bedroom without injury, but it is no way to travel through life. Sadly, we often embrace the darkness by telling ourselves things that are not true. I want to point out three instances when embracing the darkness not only slows the healing process, but it is also downright detrimental to our mental and spiritual wellbeing. Then, we'll look at how we might sow light in such places of darkness and what will be required of us to do so.

## I Am the Only One

When we suffer, we often do so in private, and it is easy to begin to be-lieve that we are the only one who has ever experienced what we are going through or who feels the way we do. And since this is something experi-enced exclusively by us, we tell ourselves, we begin to believe that there must be something wrong with us. It is a lie, of course, but such deep feelings of guilt (we have done something wrong) can easily usher in a nasty case of shame (there must be something wrong with us). And shame is hard to deal with—really hard, and it is hard on us, too. It takes us to a very dark place, and it will leave us there to struggle to find our way—with arms outstretched, hoping to avoid the wall that we imagine is somewhere right in front of us.

## I Am All Alone

In addition to the dark place of feeling like we're the only one to experience our difficulties, the dark room next door invites the notion that we're all alone. That is, there is no one who can help us, no one who really cares about us, no one to walk with us, no one who understands, and there are no resources at our disposal to assist us. We are in it all by ourselves, and we have to make our own way. Such loneliness is really a dark place, and it can quickly and easily lead to discouragement (and worse), isolation, and bouts of helplessness. At the very time when we are most in need of others, we cut ourselves off from those who love us and want to help. We shut the blinds, turn off our phones, and turn on the TV. It is a dark place, indeed.

## This Will Never End

Along with feelings of loneliness and helplessness, the darkness of hopelessness rears its ugly head. We are alone, no one can help us, *and* no matter what we try to do, our situation will never change, we tell ourselves—and we believe the lies we tell. Feeling such hopelessness is a very dark place. It robs us of any desire to lean into our situation, look for alternative strategies, or ask for help. Rather, the voices tell us, since it will never end, all we can do is sit back and endure. Motivation and hope go out the window, and all we see is the darkness creeping in.

## Is There a Witness?

Believing that we are the only one to ever experience a difficulty, that we are all alone without assistance of any kind, and that what we face will never go away are lies that we tell ourselves, and they lead us into the paralysis of the dark. So, when we pray to sow light where there is darkness, what are we praying for? What can we do? The simple answer is that we can be witnesses. To paraphrase the great author, James Baldwin, *we can stand as witnesses that swimming in deep water and drowning are not the same thing.*[2] We can shine a light into the darkness by telling our own stories and by simply saying, "Me, too. I've been where you are. You are not alone, and you will survive this. There are better seasons ahead." When we do, we confront the lies that seem to be so believable. We shine a light in the darkness because we know that just a little bit of light can dispel a great deal of darkness.

Of course, we Christians are not very good at sharing our own difficulties and failings. We don't make the best witnesses because the Christian community is not very good at knowing how to lament or tell our stories. After all, how can we share that we've been in a dark place or that we're in the dark right now if we're supposed to be perfect, that Jesus has made everything better or made all the darkness simply go away? We show up at church events with a smile and tell others that we're fine, even when we're not, which is most of us at one time or another. We haven't been encouraged or taught how to be helpfully and humbly engaging. In an upcoming section, "Practicing the Prayer of St. Francis," we'll look at several spiritual practices that will assist all of us in becoming better witnesses.

For now, however, let's finish with a quote from Jesus' Sermon on the Mount: "You are the light of the world. A town built on a hill cannot be hidden. Neither do people light a lamp and put it under a bowl. Instead they

2. Baldwin, "Sonny's Blues," 437.

put it on its stand, and it gives light to everyone in the house. In the same way, let your light shine before others" (Matt 5:14–16a). If we want to sow light where there is darkness, we can be witnesses to the darkness we have experienced in our own lives and how the Light has overcome the darkness.

## Living the Life

As a teenager, I had dreams of playing one day in the NBA, and I watched my NBA heroes on TV every weekend during the season. I remember one All-Star Weekend in particular when there was an exhibition game for former greats. I couldn't wait to see them in action, but when they took the court, I was shocked and deeply disappointed. When I saw my heroes in their late thirties, forties, and early fifties, they were . . . how should I say it . . . fat. They were out of shape, overweight, and terribly slow. They couldn't run or jump. I remembered these former players as they were in their prime, but that was gone. Of course, time had something to do with it. We all slow down as we age, but this looked to be the result of not keeping up with the disciplines in the gym or away from the refrigerator.

We all know the difference when athletes are in form and when they are not. The difference in what they are able to do is like night and day, like darkness and light. I wonder what it might mean to be "in form" spiritually, to live a life that is pleasing to God, and what it might look like to be spiritually out of form—out of shape, overweight, and terribly slow.

I want to suggest that being in spiritual form has a great deal to do with the practices we consistently undertake each day, the routines that shape us as we strive to live a well-ordered life. And the key is *daily* exercise. One does not train for a 10K race, or for any race for that matter, without a persistent, consistent, steadfast practice schedule. At the end of the day, we become what we practice.

Most of us have heard of "thin places," places like the Redwoods or the ocean where heaven and earth seem to be very close. The beauty allows the spiritual world to sneak into our daily lives. We are encouraged to seek them out. I wonder if it is possible to see it the other way around. Could we live in such a way that our daily lives meld with the spiritual, a state that I would call holy living? Others since ancient times have described it as a life that pleases God, a well-ordered life.

Let me suggest a daily practice that I have come to believe invites the Spirit to be an ever-present guest—*bookending our day*. That is, beginning each day with intention and ending it with gratitude. The practice begins by finding a quiet time each morning when we humbly pray to be vigilant to see God at work that day, to see and hear God's voice in our daily activities, and to respond accordingly when we do. It is a daily commitment to have spiritual eyes and ears. When I arrived at my office at the university each morning, I took the first fifteen minutes to pray and listen for God's voice. I didn't even look at email or check for messages. I asked God to connect all the events of the day and to reveal himself, even in the tough conversations with my boss. I used the Ignatian practice of voicing "God is present" throughout the day, whether at a celebration, a hiring, or a critical conversation with a colleague. I wanted to see and hear from God, and I wanted to live as a witness that every part of the day was holy—all of it. There was no sacred–secular divide.

And at the end of the day, my wife and I would take time to reflect on the day and share where we saw God at work in our lives and in our daily work. We also shared the three best parts of our day and gave thanks for God's presence, care, grace, and love. We bookended each day by starting with the intention to see and hear from God and ended each day with expressions of gratitude for God's care. We still do. It has become a daily practice, one that has shaped us in ways known and unknown, remembered and forgotten, and this simple routine has invited us to see God's fingerprints all over our lives, every day, not just on Sundays or on a vacation walk along the beach. A life that pleases God is a well-ordered life—one that is centered around the practice of walking with the Spirit each day.

Of course, there are many other spiritual practices that help to order our spiritual lives and shape us in God's image—contemplative prayer, meditation, journaling, the study of Scripture and other formative texts, and service to others, to name just a few—but I highly recommend bookending as a daily practice because it is easy to practice each day, anywhere, and it begins and ends our days with a spiritual focus. Moreover, bookending can easily be combined with other spiritual practices such as prayer (reciting the prayer of St. Francis, for example), devotional or lectionary readings, or waiting in silence, asking God to speak to us. And, finally, bookending is easy to explain to others who are seeking order in their own spiritual walk.

A physical education professor was once asked to identify the very best exercise that a person can do. "Any one you'll do," was his wise answer. I think the same can be said for spiritual practices. It is the consistent, intentional, daily disciplines that shape us. Any one you'll do.

Before I suggest some practical ways to sow light where there is darkness, let's look at a story from John dealing with coming to Jesus in the dark.

## SCRIPTURE

The writer of the Gospel of John tells the story of Nicodemus, a Pharisee and member of the Jewish ruling council, who came to talk with Jesus at night (John 3:1–21). He and Jesus entered into a long and often confusing discussion (on Nicodemus's part) about being born again, seeing the kingdom of God, coming into the light, living by the truth, and believing in Jesus. It is a conversation that moved from darkness to light, from blindness to sight, and from night to day, three metaphors that the writer of John's Gospel was fond of using to illustrate how one comes to belief: "But whoever lives by the truth comes into the light" (John 3:21a).

Many sermons take Nicodemus to task for coming at night, worried about being associated with Jesus' cause. In other words, he was afraid of the light and comfortable in the darkness. There is, of course, much to be gleaned from this reading of the text, but I see it slightly differently. Honestly, we don't know why Nicodemus came in the dark of night, but we do know this: he was in the dark—literally and spiritually. He was trying to find his way, believe in the truth, and live a life that was pleasing to God, as we all aspire to do, but he couldn't see clearly how to do it. Obviously, his current religious approach, although garnering much status and influence, left much to be desired. So, even in the dark, perhaps because he was in the dark and he knew it, he came to Jesus to talk with him. Jesus told him that he (Jesus) was the Light of the world, and whosoever believes in him should not perish but have eternal life. Jesus was his lamppost.

We don't know all that happened to Nicodemus after that night, but we find him mentioned two other times in John's Gospel. He cautioned that the chief priests and Pharisees should give Jesus a fair hearing before they condemned him. They didn't like it a bit (John 7:50–52). And after the crucifixion, he accompanied Joseph of Arimathea to claim and bury Jesus' body. He brought along a mixture of myrrh and aloes weighing about seventy-five pounds! That was an enormous quantity, fit for a king, enough for a royal burial (John 19:38–42). It looks like Nicodemus moved from walking in the darkness to seeing the Light.

## PRACTICING THE PRAYER OF ST. FRANCIS

As we pray to sow light where there is darkness, here are three very simple but effective ways to sow the light. First, *break bread together.* Offer a simple meal, even if it only soup and bread. There is something spiritual about gathering around a table and sharing a meal. In my view, hospitality is a practice full of grace.

Second, when you gather, *ask sincere questions*. It is easy to let an afternoon coffee or the evening be filled with small talk and table games. Of course, there is nothing wrong with small talk and table games as long as there is also time for a serious conversation or two. In my experience, honest spiritual conversations begin with a few well-intentioned questions, questions that go beyond the changing weather and the price of tomorrow's corn. Take some time in advance and think of several questions for each guest. Write them down if that will help. Almost everyone I know is honored and humbled when their opinions and stories are taken seriously. I know that I am.

Finally, *tell your story*. We all have one, and when we are honest about our own doubts and fears and failings, others usually say, "Me, too." It connects. We do stand as witnesses that swimming in deep water and drowning are not the same thing, and it is some of the best news anyone will ever hear when they are struggling to find their way home in the dark.

## A FINAL THOUGHT

Intending to sow light where there is darkness is an act of faith; sowing light by sharing our own stories is an act of grace.

## QUESTIONS FOR REFLECTION AND DISCUSSION

1. Can you think of a time when someone kept you from heading off into a thicket and losing your way? What was the result?

2. If you were to seek direction and guidance right now for a major decision in your life, to whom would you turn? Why?

3. Who are (or were) the spiritual role models in your life? What makes their lives so compelling?

4. When you are facing difficulties, which lie are you most likely to tell yourself: I'm the only one with this trouble, I am all alone, or this season will never end? Why so?

5. Why do such simple things as offering a meal, sharing your story, and asking sincere questions have such a powerful spiritual impact on others—and on us?

The Prayer of St. Francis
*Lord, make me an instrument of your peace.*
*Where there is hatred, let me sow love;*
*Where there is injury, pardon;*
*Where there is doubt, faith;*
*Where there is despair, hope;*
*Where there is darkness, light;*

# 6

## Sowing Joy Where There Is Sadness

*The Practice of Presence*

Your sadness is a gift. Don't reject it. Don't rush it. Live it fully and use it as fuel to change and grow.

—MAXIME LAGRACÉ

### INTRODUCTION

At first glance, sowing joy where there is sadness doesn't seem to be on the same plane with sowing love where there is hatred or sowing hope where there is despair, and it probably isn't. Most of us are sad at one time or another, but I must admit, I can't remember being sad as a child—not at all. Now, I grant that it might just be my memory. There are many things I don't remember from my childhood, and as my brothers will quickly attest, some of the things I do remember didn't happen at all or at least not the way I remember them.

And my family was not too much for sharing feelings of any kind. My parents were both raised on small farms during the depression, and their attitude toward loss and disappointment (I'm sure they experienced a great deal of both) was "no use crying over spilt milk" and "keep a stiff upper lip." They probably didn't even know what a stoic was, but nevertheless they were stoics, so expressing sadness wasn't something that was modeled for us at home. We were to keep our feelings to ourselves and our noses to the grindstone. My parents loved sayings such as these, and they shared them with us every chance they could, which was quite often.

Over the years, however, and especially as I neared my own retirement, sadness became a more frequent visitor, a friend even. It was a sad day when my parents died, about three years apart. I realized that our family's central station was gone, along with the homeplace. I knew that they prayed for my brothers and me by name every morning—without fail. Now I wondered if anyone prayed for me at all. And every Sunday afternoon, I would call home to "check in," as did my brothers as well. I received a report from my mother on all the family activities and events along with the news about anyone in our town or church that she thought I might remember. She was the glue that kept our family unit together and in touch. Now that the communication center was gone, I had no idea how to recreate it. Losing this family routine made me quite sad, and I would think about it often. I still do. The family anchor was gone.

I was hit with a second wave of sadness about five years before I retired. I stepped down from a senior administrative position at the university to take a teaching position. I would spend the final years of my career in the college classroom. Honestly, I loved teaching and I loved my students, but my professional identity was wrapped up with being a university administrator on a bigger stage, the way I had thought of myself for the past forty years. It was quickly and quietly gone in less than a month. As a young dean, I made a concerted effort to avoid spending much time with administrators who, at the end of their careers, would be delighted to regale me with old war stories about what it was like "back then." Suddenly, I was one of them! Losing my connections, my status, my office, my calendar, and, most importantly, my identity, made me sad—for the way I was being treated and for the ways I had treated others in the past.

I was hit with a third wave of sadness several years later. While losing one's parents and retiring from a profession one loves are events that you might expect would bring a degree of sadness, this third wave came unexpectedly out of the blue, like a sneaker wave. It was a form of ghosting—ending a personal relationship with someone by suddenly and without explanation withdrawing from all communication. Ghosting often refers to the sudden withdrawal from a dating relationship without warning, but it can also refer to ongoing relationships that end without explanation. Over the past decade, my wife and I invested heavily in young couples and single adults in our community and church—having them in our home for dinner, recommending them for leadership positions at the church, co-leading small groups, serving as mentors and advisors, and supporting and encouraging them in their own endeavors. However, when I left the provost's office and my wife resigned from her job on the pastoral staff, we became invisible. Except for one or maybe two couples, we lost all contact—no calls, no texts, no invitations, no updates, no visits, nothing. And if we would happen to see one of them at the grocery store, we would have a brief and distant conversation in passing, along with the comment that "we must get together soon," although we knew even then that it wouldn't happen. You think back and wonder: What was all that investment of our time and resources about anyway?

And most of us can think of a time when we had a very close relationship with a friend or a couple or a family, but now there is only silence. Things just drifted apart. Perhaps we were ghosted, or we did the ghosting. In either case, such memories can bring sadness for what was but is no longer, and usually there is little that can be done to make it like it was. Thomas Wolfe, in a well-known book title, recognized that it's hard to go home again.

Three personal waves of sadness, not life-shattering, but painful nonetheless. I think most of us have our own waves of sadness to navigate from time to time, or we are walking with someone who does. So, what exactly is sadness, how do we navigate these waves that are so common in life, and how do we sow joy where there is sadness in its midst? We'll address these questions next. As we will see, it is sometimes possible to gain both sadness and joy from the same experience.

## Sadness

Sadness, in some way or another, is a request for help. This can be a cue from others that they need comforting or an emotional reminder to ourselves that we need to take some time, reflect, and recoup from what we have experienced or what we are experiencing at the present moment. Sadness often cycles through periods of protest, resignation, and helplessness—accompanied by a good cry or two from time to time. It is important to note, however, that sadness is different from depression, a common but serious psychological disorder with recurrent, persistent, and intense feelings of sorrow and hopelessness that interfere with daily living. Dealing effectively with depression usually requires some kind of professional assistance, whereas, in most cases, sadness can be addressed with the wisdom and support of a good friend or two—and time.

The universal trigger for sadness is a loss of something personally important or valuable. Common sadness triggers include rejection by a friend or family member, endings and goodbyes, sickness or death of a loved one, the loss of some aspect of our identity, times of transition, and the disappointment of an unexpected outcome (like not getting that promotion you so much wanted).

Sadness, even when it is subtle, tells us that something important is happening or has happened, that it involves loss, and that some form of comforting is in order. However, recognizing sadness doesn't tell us whether we are the right person to give that comforting or who might offer comfort to us, and what form and timing that comfort might take to be helpful. In some situations, simply acknowledging that we are sorry for another person's loss and that we will be mindful of their situation in our prayers can be helpful, whereas for others it may seem like a silly, simplistic spiritual dodge.

So, what should we do? What can we do? Obviously, when we pray to sow joy where there is sadness, wisdom and spiritual understanding are in order, but how do we proceed when we try to help others or understand our own situation? I believe the epigraph at the beginning of this chapter offers us a good playbook to follow as we work to put feet to our prayers: *Your sadness is a gift. Don't reject it. Don't rush it. Live it fully and use it as fuel to change and grow.*

## Sadness Is a Gift

I know of no way to avoid being sad from time to time. There is no vaccine to protect us, no exercise routine to prevent it, no family system to defend us, and no way to reason it away. It is one of the basic human emotions, and since we are all human, there we are. And honestly, I'm not sure we should avoid sadness even if we could. As it turns out, it is an uninvited visitor with hidden benefits. Sadness is not a punishment from God or a sign of human weakness, and there is no shame in feeling sad. The shame is in the rejection of the opportunity it affords us.

We know that sadness comes during times of loss or transition, signaling that something important has happened or is happening, and that comforting of one kind or another is in order. Sadness, then, is a gift, giving us the opportunity to be introspective, to pay attention to the less-visited side streets of our lives, to carefully ask honest questions, to go deep, and to gain a new perspective about what is going on around us, whether we are dealing with our own sadness or walking with someone who is.

*Don't Reject It*

We can choose to accept sadness as a gift, albeit an uninvited one, and act accordingly for our own benefit and the benefit of those around us, or we can choose to see sadness as something else—a curse, a personal character flaw, a sign of weakness, even a punishment from God. Moreover, we can simply act as if we are feeling nothing at all, the old "grin and bear it" strategy, and we can hope that the sadness will just go away of its own accord. The logic behind such behaviors is that unacknowledged feelings cannot do any harm. Sadly, that is simply poor logic. When we deny our feelings, they find a way to the surface, and rarely to our benefit.

*Don't Rush It*

Sometimes we don't reject sadness patently out of hand, but we try to put our feelings on a schedule or postpone them until a more convenient time. "Tomorrow is Linda's birthday," we tell ourselves, "so I can only be sad until 4:40 this afternoon," or "I'll have a good cry when this is all over, but not now. There is too much cleanup to do." However, sadness comes without invitation, with its own timetable, and with no "use by" date stamped on the package. There is no next day guaranteed delivery from sadness. It takes time—and holy patience.

*Live It Fully and Use It*

If we shouldn't try to ignore sadness, or reject it, or hide it, or rush it, then what can we do when sadness comes? Good question, indeed. I've always loved the old popular saying, *If you can't get out of it, get into it!* I believe that this applies to our sadness, too. The key is to get into it, to live it fully. We can name sadness for what it is, we can embrace it as a friend, and we can talk about it honestly and openly.

Feeling sad can be used as an invitation to be introspective, to learn, and to pay attention to what is going on in our own lives and in the lives of those we love. We can acknowledge the sadness, accepting it as a gift and a bidding to grow and go deeper in our relationships with God and with each other. We can deal with sadness as a spiritual discipline, one that shapes and forms us as we make the journey we call life-together.

## SCRIPTURE

"Weeping may stay for the night, but rejoicing comes in the morning," the psalmist writes (Ps 30:5b). Many Bible translations use "joy" instead of "rejoicing." Honestly, I like that better. Joy comes in the morning, and sometimes through our mourning. Out of the darkness of the night comes the Light; out of the weeping comes joy. It isn't an instant turnaround or a quick fix or a magic trick. It takes patience, insight, comfort, and time, but joy does come.

As it turns out, joy is both a state of mind (a feeling) and an orientation of the heart. At its spiritual core, joy is a settled state of contentment, confidence, and hope. It is a deeply rooted expression of our confidence in God's goodness and presence. That's why joy and peace are so closely related, sometimes thought of as twins—each different but sharing the same DNA. So, when we pray to sow joy where there is sadness, it is a spiritual challenge to look for ways to bring comfort and to share the good news that God is present, always—and God is good.

When Jesus appeared to his disciples after his resurrection, he told them three times, "Peace be with you" (John 20:19, 21, 26). Why? Because they were afraid, confused, and sad. That's why. Who wouldn't be? They were in desperate need of comfort. By sharing God's peace with his closest friends, Jesus modeled for us the power of sharing confidence in God's goodness and presence. And what was the result? A settled state of contentment, confidence, and hope. In other words—joy. Not a giddy, giggly veneer of happiness, but a deep joy in a God who is the keeper of promises. A joy deep enough to stay faithful, to face trials, abuse, even death, and to build the church.

Of course, we are seldom called upon to face such dire circumstances, but the confidence, contentment, and hope that Jesus shared with his disciples can be taken to heart when we are sad, and it can be shared with our neighbors, too. Perhaps that is what it means to love our neighbors as ourselves. We start by sharing God's peace, sowing joy where there is sadness.

## PRACTICING THE PRAYER OF ST. FRANCIS

If we know that sadness, in some way or another, tells us that something important is happening or has happened, that it involves loss, and that some form of comforting is in order, what are some practical ways to practice the prayer of St. Francis? What comfort can we offer beyond sharing our understanding of the sadness process and the assurance that joy comes in the morning? Let me list three simple offerings. I think you can connect the dots and see the big picture. Comfort comes in a variety of shapes and sizes, and although they are simple, they are sacred, too.

## Use a Table

I can think of few things as powerful and nothing more comforting, more holy, than breaking bread together. So, when we want to offer comfort to a friend, use a table. That is, find time to share a coffee or a simple meal together, and if that is not possible, take them a meal. Comfort will be present even in your absence. I am not sure why offering some food and fellowship is so powerful, but I know that it is. It can provide time for sacred conversations, whether through laughter, through tears, or in holy silence. The table is an instrument of God's grace.

## Take a Walk

There is also something comforting about taking a walk together, whether in a beautiful forest setting or just around the neighborhood. When we walk side by side, we are looking in the same direction, so while we are close, we are not directly staring at each other's face. We stop trying to read facial expressions or hide our own. This provides both a sense of intimacy and a sense of privacy that is conducive to honest and holy conversations. Often the memory of a thirty-minute walk can linger for an entire week, even longer. A walk is an instrument of God's grace.

## Commit to the Journey

Finally, while we know that sadness is more temporary than depression and often fades with time, there is no set timetable for this sadness journey. One of the best ways to offer comfort to a friend is to sign up for the journey. That is, make an appointment to meet each Thursday afternoon for a coffee or a walk for the next six weeks, or a promise that you will call them every other day for the next two weeks. When we are sad, there is great comfort in knowing that someone cares and we are not alone. Of course, often the sadness lifts before the commitments have reached their end. What a great opportunity to give thanks together and to talk about where life is taking us now and what we can learn from the journey. The promise of persistent presence is an instrument of God's grace, too.

## A FINAL THOUGHT

I have shared many a coffee or simple meal with a suffering soul, and sometimes I have been the one doing the suffering. I have come to believe that whenever we meet and share some nourishment and spend some honest time together, it tastes a little bit, just a little bit, like bread and wine. It is a sacramental moment filled with grace.

## QUESTIONS FOR REFLECTION AND DISCUSSION

1. Can you think of the last time you were sad, really sad? What was the trigger—loss, disappointment, or something else? How long did the sadness last, and how were you able to move on?

2. It seems that most of us have been ghosted at one time or another, or we have ghosted someone else. Why is ghosting much more common than we would like to admit? What might be done about it?

3. Why is offering a simple meal such a holy activity, filled with grace? What makes it so?

4. If you were to go on a walk with a troubled friend, where would you go? Why there?

5. Can you recall a time when someone came alongside you and was committed to your journey? How might we return the favor or pay it forward?

The Prayer of St. Francis
*Lord, make me an instrument of your peace.*
*Where there is hatred, let me sow love;*
*Where there is injury, pardon;*
*Where there is doubt, faith;*
*Where there is despair, hope;*
*Where there is sadness, joy.*

# PART II

## Seeking the Best for Others

THERE IS A SUBTLE shift in this prayer from sowing to seeking, and in this case, seeking the best for others. Honestly, this is not as easy as it sounds. In many ways, we are oriented and pushed, urged even, to take care of number one. We live in a self-seeking society. I was amazed but not surprised when I witnessed some in my own community who gamed the system, used unauthorized channels, and cut the line to receive their COVID vaccination shots ahead of those vulnerable ones who were in a much higher-risk category for serious illness and death but played by the rules. And then to cap it off, they posted their vaccination cards on Facebook with a big smile as if they had just won the lottery. Apparently, we're better together but best when we take care of ourselves and let everyone else make their own way.

At the same time, the Prayer of St. Francis does not suggest that we are not to be consoled, not to be understood, and not to be loved. Rather, it is keeping things in proper perspective. Jesus didn't teach total denial or annihilation of self. In fact, he said that the second greatest commandment was to love our neighbor *as ourselves*. To me, that is a fine balance that can be extremely difficult to pull off, and certainly not in our own strength.

I think the prayer "For Today," published on the inside cover of *Forward Day by Day*, a daily devotional published by the Episcopal Church, provides some insight: "I will try this day to live a simple, sincere, and serene life, repelling promptly every thought of discontent, anxiety, discouragement, impurity, and *self-seeking*."[1] There it is again—self-seeking.

1. "For Today."

Thankfully, the prayer doesn't end there. It continues: "And since I cannot in my own strength do this, nor even with a hope of success attempt it, I look to thee, O Lord God my Father, in Jesus my Savior, and ask for the gift of the Holy Spirit." That's the key! As it turns out, it is a spiritual discipline, a holy act to put others' needs before our own without losing ourselves in the process. We learn to do this with God's help, and we get better at it as it is consistently practiced. That's why this section of St. Francis's prayer begins with these compelling words: "O Divine Master, *Grant* that I may not *so much seek* . . ." It is a powerful part of the prayer, asking our Divine Master to grant us, teach us, lead us, and shape us to be less self-seeking and more like Jesus—to be holy. And as we shall see, seeking to console has its own consolation, seeking to understand has its own wisdom, and seeking to love has its own embrace for those who pray this prayer in earnest.

# 7

## Seeking to Console

### *The Practice of Kindness*

Never allow your sorrow to absorb you, but seek out another to console, and you will find consolation.

—J. C. MACAULAY

### INTRODUCTION

In this chapter and the two that follow in Part II, we will be looking for spiritual practices that will help us to console (to see others), to understand (to hear others), and to love (to embrace others), even when we may be in deep need of the same from others. Let's face it. It is difficult to practice seeing others when it feels like no one is watching out for us. It is difficult to practice hearing others into speech when it seems that no one is listening to us. And it is especially hard to embrace others when it seems that the whole world has pushed us away. I get that—been there, felt that way. Yet, when we pray the Prayer of St. Francis, this is exactly what we are hoping to do, or more accurately, what we are asking God to do through us and for us. We'll begin with offering consolation—seeing behind the smile that we have all learned to display, no matter how rotten our day has been or how rotten we feel about ourselves.

## I See You

No one wants to be offered a consolation prize, but consolation we'll gladly take. To console means to sympathize, to help, to aid, to support, to encourage, to reassure, to really see someone. At one time or another, we've all needed that kind of kindness. Ultimately, to console is a spiritual practice, a way of seeing others—really seeing them—and letting them know in tangible ways that we do. It takes wisdom and presence.

If we are fortunate, there are one or two persons in our lives who see right through us. We can walk in with a smile and a joke, and they'll respond, "What's wrong. I can see it written all over your face." They just see us for who we are, and we can't hide. Honestly, it is one of the most precious gifts anyone will ever receive—a friend who sees us for who we really are and not the public persona we try to fabricate as we go through our day. And when they ask, we tell the truth about ourselves! Because they see us, we open up and share the good, bad, and ugly. That is consolation in action.

## I'm Here and I'm Not Going Anywhere

I suppose that deep and honest conversations can happen with a perfect stranger. Sometimes there is a sense of safety in sharing our stuff with someone we don't know and won't ever see again, but I think that something very important, very spiritual, can be lost when such reality-challenging, potentially life-changing interactions, transpire with someone who has not walked the long road with us and won't be with us for the rest of the journey. The phrase I'm searching for is *a present fellowship*. As the writer of 1 John puts it: "But if we walk in the light, as he is in the light, we have fellowship with one another" (1 John 1:7). Walking in the light is hard at any time, but it's much easier with someone who has seen our darkest moments and is still there for the long daylight journey ahead. One of the most powerful spiritual disciplines we can practice when we pray to offer consolation is to simply see others for who they are, not for the persons we wish they would be, and then demonstrate time and time again that we are for them and with them for the long haul. We're here and we're not going anywhere.

## Hey, What about Me?

But how do we practice a present fellowship with others when we're in bad shape, too, have been through the ringer, and are uncertain what the next day or week might bring our way? How do we see others in their time of need when we do not see a way forward for ourselves? How do we seek not so much to be consoled as to console? Let's be honest. It is easy to mouth these words as we repeat St. Francis's prayer in unison on Sunday, but where do we find the spiritual strength and wisdom to see others in need of consolation when we are hurting, too? Must we ignore our own lives when we minister to others? Thankfully, the answer is no. I deeply believe that consolation will come to us, will find us, often at unexpected times and in unexpected ways. I hope the following personal story will illustrate this reality.

## Going Home for Consolation

The four-hour drive back to the homeplace seemed like an eternity. It was a familiar trip in many ways. I'd driven it dozens of times, but today seemed like an endless journey to nowhere. I didn't want to arrive home like this, all battered and bruised, but I knew I had to go. When I was in high school, my parents would tell me that I could always come home any time, no matter how things were going, and especially if things were rotten or I was in trouble. The lights would always be on for me. That assurance alone was a great comfort to me, even though I was now long past high school and on my own for more years as I had spent at home. I was one of those who graduated from college and never looked back—and returned home only for a holiday every other year or so.

Even though I didn't see them very often, I knew that my folks were very proud of me. I had been busy going to graduate school and establishing a career, making more money in my first year after college than my dad would ever make in any year of his life. I knew that they prayed for me every single day after breakfast, and that they cared deeply about how I was doing, but I rarely took the opportunity to share the interior of my life with them. I mostly shared my successes.

Now, I must admit that it had never been easy to talk to my parents adult-to-adult. My father grew up on a small, struggling bean farm, and his fundamentalist parents weren't much for conversations of any kind, insisting instead that everyone would do well to keep their proverbial noses to the grindstone and refuse to cry over spilt milk. On one occasion when I was home for Christmas, I found my father sitting quietly in the living room. "Dad," I said, "I have just finished reading an inspiring passage from one of my favorite authors who really speaks my language." I shared the passage with him. He looked at me for what seemed like an eternity, and then said, "They are building a new overpass on the freeway outside of town. Do you have any idea how often hydraulics come into play when building a bridge of any sort?" I had to admit that I didn't; hydraulics wasn't my specialty. He suggested that that would be a good thing to read about if I had some spare time. So much for a conversation with my dad about my interior life.

My mother, on the other hand, was a bit more of a conversationalist but had a way of turning the subject back to her own frame of reference—or sideways. She asked once what all the fuss was about those comprehensive exams for my doctorate. I explained to her that writing comprehensive exams, which lasted three long, excruciating days, was the step between finishing years of coursework and writing a research dissertation. I explained to her in detail the scope of the exams, the months of preparation it took, how I managed my time over the three days, what I did each evening to recuperate, and the unbelievable sense of relief I had when, after meeting with my doctoral committee two weeks later to defend my writing, they said that I had passed with honors and talked with me about my intentions for the dissertation. It was a glowing success, and the proudest moment of my academic career thus far. I shared it all with a deep sense of satisfaction.

Mother nodded her head in approval and said, "Now that is *exactly* like what happened to me last week. It was time to renew my driver's license. I drove over the Ithaca [a town about six miles away] and picked up a booklet. I studied it for an hour in the parking lot, and then took the test. It consisted of ten questions that I had to answer using a computer screen. It was tense, but I passed on the first try, so I know *exactly* what you are talking about. It is always good to pass a test on the first try!"

"Yup," I said, "*exactly*" with a note to self—no more talk about doctoral work with the family.

Notwithstanding my family's lack of experience with sharing feelings of any kind and my own experience with trying to share my interior life with my folks, I needed to come home—I had to come home. To be honest, I didn't have anywhere else to go. Although my professional career was an impressive tale of one upward move after another and I was doing quite well in my current job as a senior administrator at a fine Christian university, my personal life was in the toilet. Out of the blue, I was served with divorce papers over the Christmas holidays. It came as a complete surprise to me. Looking back, it probably shouldn't have been, but it was. I honestly didn't know what to do. Everyone seemed to be aware of my "situation," but no one stepped forward to offer any direction or comfort of any sort that I can remember. The university had a conservative element of support that began to call for my resignation. For them, divorce was a sign of moral failure and spiritual weakness of one kind or another. I began to fear that I would lose my job, a major part of my identity. I wondered if I should just go away and never come back, but where would I go?

It was in this state of mind that I started for home. While driving up the freeway, I rehearsed my speech to my parents, having them sit down in the living room and informing them of the state of my marriage and the storm clouds hovering over my job and even my career. I don't know what I expected them to say or do, but since they always said that I could come home anytime, even if how I was doing was rotten, I thought I would take them up on their evergreen invitation. Clearly, I had the rotten part down.

As was her custom, my mother had a meal prepared for me when I arrived. Even though it was in the middle of the afternoon, she just knew that I would be hungry. So, we ate a huge lunch—all three of us. My dad always went along with the custom, never complaining about an extra meal. While we were sitting at the table making small talk, I casually asked how things were going at church. They looked at each other and suddenly burst into tears. This was totally unexpected. One long-standing family custom was that we didn't talk about our feelings; the other was that crying was out of the question. Here they were, crying and trying to express how rotten they felt. I listened and asked a few questions along the way. That's all it took. We sat at the table until long after dark.

To give you some context, church was always very important to our family, and when I say church, I mean the local church in our hometown. They grew up in that church, were married there, dedicated their children there, and buried their parents there. My dad oversaw the construction of the new church building out on the highway, one of the highlights of his life. At one time or another, they held almost every conceivable position: teacher, youth leader, music director, missionary coordinator, head usher, treasure, janitor, and Sunday school superintendent. They were "all in" and had been so for their entire lives.

However, it all changed when a new pastor came to the church. He announced that the new focus of the church would be on families with young children, even though there was a large and active Senior Adult Ministries group. The pastor promptly fired the SAMs minister, a very close friend of my parents. They often referred to him as one of their boys, showing how much they cared for him as he ministered to them. He was suddenly gone. When my dad protested at the next board meeting (he served as the chair of the board), he was told by the pastor that he needed to step down from the board, and it would be better if he and mom attended another church. They were no longer welcome if they couldn't get with the program—his program. They staggered away in total disbelief, and although they were attending a small church in the next town, they were left with anger, hurt, and a total sense of abandonment. My mother put it this way: "We go to church, but we feel like nomads. We don't belong anywhere."

Over the next two days, they poured out their hearts to me. Even though I had come home in deep need of comfort, I was now the one doing the comforting. As it turns out, they had no one to talk to either, and their entire life of faith had been turned upside down. It was a long and painful conversation, but as we cried, laughed, prayed, and remembered so many good times at church, I reassured them that new life would come in due time, but it would take time. It did, but it did.

A few days later as I headed back down the freeway, I knew that these conversations with my parents in their time of need were sacred moments—for them and for me. I have come to believe that God works in mysterious ways, and that weekend was truly one of those mysteries. I came in need of comfort, offered comfort instead, and left knowing deep within my spirit that I had been comforted, too, even though I didn't share a word about my own messy life that weekend. I left with a deep assurance that new life would come my way, too, in due time, but it would take time. It did, but it did. Others stepped into my life, and I did find my way—or more truthfully, Way found me. Thanks be to God.

## SCRIPTURE

"Praise be to the God and Father of our Lord Jesus Christ, the Father of compassion and the God of all comfort, who comforts us in all our troubles, so that we can comfort those in any trouble with the comfort we ourselves receive from God" (2 Cor 1:3–4). The Father of compassion and the God of all comfort—I love this expression of God's love for us, which we, in turn, share with suffering souls around us. Some versions refer to God as the Father of mercies. I love that, too. When we seek to console others, we do not do so with our own limited resources. That would be like approaching the ocean of grace with a teaspoon.

Instead, as Paul suggests, we extend to others that which God has extended to us, that which we, all of us, have personally experienced. And what is God's nature that we experience and share in times of trouble of one kind or another? I believe the book of Lamentations puts it best, and who should know more about experiencing and expressing troubles than the prophet Jeremiah? He wasn't called the weeping prophet for nothing, yet this is his conclusion: "The steadfast love of the LORD never ceases; his mercies never come to an end; they are new every morning; great is your faithfulness. 'The LORD is my portion,' says my soul, 'therefore I will hope in him'" (Lam 3:22–24 ESV).

We can draw out five points of experience from Jeremiah's affirmation of God's character: God's love is steadfast, steady, and there's nothing we can do to make God stop loving us—nothing; his mercies never stop coming our way—never; we can sense renewal in the mercies of God each morning—each day can be a fresh start; and God is faithful—period. When I speak to college students or senior citizens, I usually end in the same way: "There are two things you can count on: one is that life is messy—it either has been, is, or will be; but you can count on this, too—God is faithful. His mercies are new each morning, his love never ceases, great is his faithfulness unto us, and as the mountains surround Jerusalem, so the Lord surrounds his people both now and forever. Amen? Amen!"

Finally, we can all join with Jeremiah in proclaiming, "The LORD is our portion, we will hope in him." And it is this hope that we share when we attempt of console others, and it is this truth that consoles us as we do.

## PRACTICING THE PRAYER OF ST. FRANCIS

Various spiritual practices have been suggested throughout this chapter, so we'll let this section serve as a summary or reminder of what practical steps we might take when we earnestly pray that we might not seek so much to be consoled as to console others. Admittedly, it isn't always easy to do, but what part of this prayer is? And like other spiritual disciplines, we do get better with practice.

## Focus on Others

I believe the first step is to be intentional about seeing others who need consolation of one kind or another, and there are many ways to console. It might be a kind word, a compliment, a helping hand, a meal, a ride, a blessing, or a promise that you are there for the long haul. The key is to have eyes that see and to respond accordingly without making yourself or your situation the center of it all. Honestly, that's always a temptation, especially when we are hurting, too, so it takes real discipline to keep our own experience and needs on the sidelines and focus on others. But when we consistently do, there is a payoff that comes back to us. As I wrote earlier in this chapter, I can't explain how it works. It is a spiritual mystery, but a spiritual truism, too. When we focus on loving our neighbors, we end up loving ourselves, too, or opening ourselves up to receive the love of others. It is a mystery of grace.

## Walk with God

The idea of walking with the Spirit is referenced at least fifteen times in Scripture. My favorite comes in Galatians right after the apostle Paul lists out the fruit of the Spirit (love, joy, peace, forbearance, kindness, gentleness, and self-control). He then urges his readers and all of us: "Since we live by the Spirit, let us keep in step with the Spirit" (Gal 5:25). In other words, don't just stand there, walk! Certainly, it's hard to keep in step with anything if we just stand there and watch the parade. So, how do we walk with the Spirit—with God? We keep our eyes and ears open, and we search for opportunities to console others, knowing that we do not do so in our own strength, wisdom, and insight. Rather, we're on a spiritual mission to offer grace, healing, and comfort to our neighbors, to those we encounter along the way as we do our best to keep in step with the Spirit. We head out ready to enter the arena rather than to take a reserved seat in the first row. And as we do, the mystery is that the Spirit keeps in step with us, too! As we offer our presence to others, God's presence is there—for us, with us, and in us. We don't walk for God; we walk with God and draw from an ocean of grace as we do.

## When Consolation Comes Full Circle, Embrace It

I have alluded several times in this chapter to the mystery that happens when we seek to console others—consolation comes our way, too. I don't know how it happens, but I know that it does. It is so easy, however, to fail to recognize grace and healing when it comes our way or to reject it because we feel unworthy, shrugging it off as unnecessary attention. No matter how we feel at the time, we need to accept and embrace comfort when it comes our way, knowing what a gift of grace it truly is.

Sometimes the love of God hits us right in the face, but we fail to recognize the obvious. There is an old story from the Northwest about a man who was wanting to see a sign from God—any sign. Just then, an eagle flew by carrying a goose. The eagle released the goose, and the goose flew down and landed in front of the man. As it did, she flapped her wings and out flew a charm of hummingbirds, spelling in big letters: I'm here! As the man watched all of this take place, he continued to pray: "Just give me a sign—any sign." I wonder if we are sometimes guilty of the same response to God's grace. We pray to God for eyes to see and ears to hear how we might minister to others, but when God's grace comes our way, we turn blind and deaf.

All this to say, when consolation comes our way, let us have the insight, courage, and humility to thankfully accept it. Honestly, it is one of the hardest spiritual disciplines to practice.

## A FINAL THOUGHT

If we are committed to practicing the Prayer of St. Francis, we will be challenged and stretched in ways known and unknown, but we will also experience some of the mysteries of the faith, not the least of which is that when we seek more to console than to be consoled, the road runs both ways. All we are asked to do is pay attention and walk with the Spirit; God will do the heavy lifting.

## QUESTIONS FOR REFLECTION AND DISCUSSION

1. When you seek to console someone, what is your go-to activity: a coffee, a meal, a long walk, a note, a blessing, or . . . ?

2. Can you think of the last time someone offered consolation to you? What made it so meaningful to you?

3. Can you think of someone in need of consolation who simply refused all overtures and expressions of support? What do you think was at work in this instance?

4. Why is the promise to walk the long road with someone in need of consolation so powerful, so spiritual, so helpful?

5. Have you ever prayed for God to do something in your life, to show you a sign, and then failed to recognize it when it came your way? Explain.

The Prayer of St. Francis
*Lord, make me an instrument of your peace.*
*Where there is hatred, let me sow love;*
*Where there is injury, pardon;*
*Where there is doubt, faith;*
*Where there is despair, hope;*
*Where there is darkness, light;*
*Where there is sadness, joy.*
*O Divine Master,*
*Grant that I may not so much seek*
*To be consoled as to console;*

# 8

## Seeking to Understand

### *The Practice of Listening*

Most people do not listen with the intent to understand; they listen with the intent to reply.

—STEPHEN R. COVEY

### INTRODUCTION

According to Goethe, we hear only what we understand.[1] While that may be true, I wonder if the reverse isn't true as well, perhaps even more so—we understand only what we hear. If it is, and I think it is, when we pray to understand others, we are praying first to be a better listener. Just as offering comfort requires us to see others, understanding summons us to listen others into speech, to paraphrase Parker Palmer,[2] and then to graciously hold and nurture what has been shared with us. How do we do this? Let's start with the practice of listening.

1. Goethe, "A Person Only Hears."
2. I have heard him say "listening others into speech" in person many times, including at an educational speech to the board of trustees at Point Loma Nazarene University in San Diego, California, in 2001.

## Listening

When I was twelve, I received a puppy for Christmas. His registered name was Tinker's Independent Boy because he was the first one out of the litter box. But he was soon into all kinds of things, so we just called him Troubles. As it turned out, Troubles quickly became the entire family's dog, but I always felt that we had a special connection. I remember sitting together under the silver maple tree in our back yard one hot summer's day and saying to him, "Troubles, you're the only one in this world who truly understands me." He just tilted his head and wagged his tail. Honestly, he was probably hoping for a snack of one kind or another, but he had the rudimentary skills for being a good listener down cold. He maintained eye contact, didn't interrupt, didn't react, didn't judge, and didn't offer any unsolicited advice. He just made it known that he was happy to be with me.

Now, please hear me. I am not advocating that all we must do to be good listeners is to act like the family dog (although we could do worse). However, I am saying that becoming a good listener is hard work, and we should take instruction from any source we can. As it turns out, asking a good question or two and then earnestly listening without interjecting ourselves into the conversation is one of the sincerest forms of respect we can pay someone. Karl Menninger believed that listening was a magnetic, creative force.[3] The friends who listen to us are the ones we move toward, and when we are listened to, it allows us to unfold and expand. I think he's spot on. *We move toward those who listen to us.* Here are two examples of listening—one good, one not so good—examples that either draw us in or push us away. I think the difference will be obvious.

### The Big-Time Pastor

After my sophomore year in college, I transferred to a Christian university to play basketball. As it turns out, basketball was big in that community and I became sort of a local celebrity on campus, even known by the ministerial staff at the large college church where I attended. They greeted me by name each Sunday. But something wasn't quite right. As the senior pastor made his way across the foyer after church, he would look at me, smile, shake my hand, and say, "How are you, Patrick?" He did so every Sunday, but after several weeks it dawned on me that he would be looking at me when he was greeting others as he made his way across the room, and when he spoke to me, he was already looking down the line a bit for the next person to greet.

3. Menninger, "Listening Is a Magnetic."

He would ask how I was, but it was clear that he didn't have any interest in knowing how I was doing. He had already moved on. I was simply one of the stepping-stones he used to cross the stream of people standing between himself and the front door.

One Sunday as the pastor was working the crowd, he asked me how I was doing in the usual way, and I replied, "I'm discouraged and feel like dropping out of school."

"Great! Good to see you," he said as he moved on. Over the next several weeks, I purposely offered increasingly troubling reports about how I was doing, and they were always met with the same response, "Great! Good to see you," as he moved on to the next person in his line of sight. Honestly, the insincerity and superficiality of these interactions left me feeling invisible and empty. I avoided these foyer meetings as best I could. Pretense is no substitute for friendship or fellowship.

## The Campus Pastor

The first time I met the campus pastor, I could tell that we were going to be best friends. I'm not sure if it was his smile, his humanity, his sense of kindness, or the fact that when he listened to me it was obvious that I was the only person in his entire world at that time. I had his full attention. He would ask how I was doing, and then wait for an answer. He really wanted to know. Even though he had a breakneck schedule, he would make time for me, and as it turns out, for everyone else, too. When he had a meeting across campus, he would leave his office thirty or forty minutes early because it seemed that he always ran into a person or two who "needed to talk." He always had time to listen.

The campus pastor passed away far too young, succumbing to an unrelenting brain cancer. At his funeral, I was amazed that almost everyone there described him as one of their best friends, and the reality was, he was! He took time for everyone, listening others into speech. He focused more on listening to others than on seeking to be heard, daily putting the Prayer of St. Francis into practice in a most practical way. He was fully present, and his life demonstrated that *we move toward those who listen to us.*

## Holding and Nurturing

The campus pastor was not only a good listener, but he also held what was shared closely and gently, and after a conversation with him, you could expect a follow-up note or a call or an invitation for coffee or to just hang out and play guitars. "I've been thinking and praying about what you shared last week," he would casually say as he smiled and looked me in the eyes. "So how are you feeling about all of this today? Would you like to talk about it? How can I pray for you?" He invited an honest conversation, one that led to deeper insight and genuine friendship. He was a good listener, and he carried what was shared with him as a sacred trust, always committed to nurturing a deeper understanding.

And often, I would receive a phone call, sometimes from someone I didn't even know. "I've been talking with the campus pastor," they would mention, "and he suggested that it might be a good idea for us to get together . . ." It happened more times than I can tell you.

If we want to understand others, we certainly need to learn how to listen—and to learn how to practice holy silence. Obviously, we can't gain a deep understanding of anyone if we are doing all the talking. And we not only seek to hear others into speech, we also seek to hold and nurture what has been shared with us. It is in this holy ground that understanding takes root and grows. *We move toward those who listen to us, but we walk with those who hold and nurture what we share with holy care.*

## Gaining Understanding

When we pray to understand others even *more* than we seek to be understood, it is an act of humility, a holy intention, a sacred journey—and journeys take time. The journey starts with the intent to become a better listener, and several concrete actions for doing so will be addressed in the "Practicing the Prayer of Francis" section that follows. Suffice it here to say that if we go through our days doing all the talking, pushing to be heard and promoting ourselves and our opinions, understanding will elude us—and even our friends will avoid us as best they can.

In many ways, when we seek to understand someone, it is understanding that finds us. It isn't something that we can just create from some old family recipe. Honestly, I don't know how it works—it is a holy mystery to me, but I do know that when we set aside our egos and fully focus on another, listening and holding and nurturing that which has been shared with us, something good, something real, something honest develops along the way. We begin to understand. *We move toward those who listen to us, but we walk with those who hold and nurture what we share with holy care; and as we journey together, understanding finds us and dwells among us full of grace and truth.*

## SCRIPTURE

God keeps coming to us as God has always done. God came to Abram and said, "'Go from your country, your people and your father's household to the land I will show you' . . . So Abram went" (Gen 12:1, 4a). Later, God came to Abraham and commanded him to sacrifice his son, Isaac, but provided a substitute (something I still do not fully understand to this day) (Gen 22:1–19). God came to Jacob as he slept on a stone pillow at Bethel (Gen 28:10–22). In a burning bush, God came to Moses: "When the Lord saw that he had gone over to look, God called to him from within the bush, 'Moses! Moses!' And Moses said, 'Here I am'" (Exod 3:4). God kept coming—to Joshua (Josh 1:9), to Samuel (1 Sam 3:4–16), to Elijah (1 Kgs 17:2–6), to Isaiah (Isa 1), to Jeremiah (Jer 1:4), and to Joel (Joel 1:1). I could go on and on.

We see in the New Testament that God came to Mary, Joseph, Elizabeth, and Zechariah (Matt 1; Luke 1), telling how God would come to earth in the person of Jesus. We see Jesus coming to the poor and dispossessed (Matt 11:4–6), to tax collectors (Luke 5:27–32) and prostitutes (Matt 21:31–32), and, after the crucifixion, to Mary (John 20:11–18), to the disciples (John 20:19–23), to Thomas (John 20:24–29), to the travelers on the Emmaus Road (Luke 24:13–35), and later to Peter on the shore of the Sea of Galilee (John 21:15–19), and later still to the apostle Paul on the Damascus Road (Acts 9:1–31). As promised, the Holy Spirit came on the day of Pentecost (Acts 2:1–13). God kept coming and coming and coming.

And it isn't that God comes only for the inner circle or a select few. Isaiah makes it clear that the Lord will come and seek—even the gentiles: "I revealed myself to those who did not ask for me; I was found by those who did not seek me. To a nation that did not call on my name, I said, 'Here am I, here am I'" (Isa 65:1). That's good news for all of us.

God keeps coming, and so it is, I believe, with consolation and understanding. They come to us as we seek to console and understand others. Honestly, how it all works is a spiritual mystery to me, but I have learned to embrace this mystery because that's the way God works. If we are to embrace the Prayer of St. Francis and diligently and daily put it into practice, it is a declaration of faith in a God who would not let our sin or anything else ruin the possibility of a divine relationship; it is faith in a God who keeps coming and coming and coming. And for that, we can all be thankful.

## PRACTICING THE PRAYER OF ST. FRANCIS

Just as offering consolation is a way of truly seeing someone, seeking to understand someone demands that we be listeners. It requires spiritual discipline, engaging in a set of practices that shape us even as we attempt to listen others into speech. I want to briefly discuss three of these formative practices. They may appear to be profoundly simple, but if we earnestly engage in them, I believe that they will turn out to be simply profound: offering holy silence, holding and nurturing, and seeking understanding.

## Offering Holy Silence

Silence can be deafening, and not all silence is holy. Silence can be used to ignore, to exclude, and to punish, but offering holy silence is an act of grace. As the epigram reminds us at the start of this chapter, we often listen with the intent to respond rather than to understand. Proverbs rightly calls out such behavior: "To answer before listening—that is folly and shame" (18:13).

James urges all of us to take note: "Everyone should be quick to listen, slow to speak and slow to become angry" (1:19). Quick to listen and slow to speak—that's the practice of holy silence. It is so alien in a world where the typical response to our sharing is "Do you know what you should do!" or "That's exactly what happened to me, and this is what I did. If you're smart, you'll do the same." Such responses are not holy, and they are rarely helpful.

Listening in silence is not easy, but we can get better at it with practice. When we look forward to having coffee with someone, think about the discipline and preparation it will take to listen rather than to offer advice or talk about ourselves or just talk about sports or the weather—to make the conversation about them, not about us. It is the practice of offering holy silence, and it is powerful. It takes eye contact, not a personal soliloquy.

## Holding and Nurturing

If we are fortunate enough to listen someone into speech, the great temptation is to tell others what we have heard, to share what we know. Honestly, it is a way to make us feel more important in some strange way, but it is simply a form of gossip. If we pray this prayer in earnest, we gently hold what we have heard, as if it were sacred, because in many ways, it is.

And we nurture what has been shared with us. We think about it carefully and prayerfully and privately. We wonder what that person might need most right now, what the next steps are, and what we might do to offer support or assistance. Many times, there is little we can do other than to pray and be present. That's ok, too. We offer friendship and let God do the heavy lifting. But sometimes there are things that we can do, concrete actions that will make a difference. When such a course of action is clear, we nurture what has been shared with us by humbly and cautiously speaking to someone on their behalf or working to open a door or two. Whatever we do, it must be done with spiritual sensitivity. There is no circus for us to rush in and save.

There is an implicit tension when we attempt to both hold and nurture what has been shared with us. Sometimes we are called to holy silence—we must hold. At other times, we are called to holy action—we must do something. We start by praying for the wisdom to know the difference and for integrity and courage when we do.

## Seeking Understanding

Thus far, we have examined two spiritual disciplines or practices that help us when we pray to seek to understand someone in good times and bad—to offer holy silence and to hold and nurture what has been shared with us. These practices will require our best selves, of course, but remember we are not just seeking to be a good listener or a trusted advisor. We are praying for more than that. We are seeking to understand. This is at its heart a spiritual quest, and it takes time. It is a journey, not a sprint. Understanding does not come with a two-minute conversation in the check-out line at the local grocery.

I have come to believe that all of us have three innate spiritual desires or invitations—to go deep, to be known, and to find home. We desire a deeper relationship with our Creator; we want to be known and accepted for who we really are; and we want to find our way home. I believe that different people express and pursue these desires differently, and at any one time, one of these desires is much closer to the surface. I don't think we even think about them much, but there they are. When we embrace someone with the desire to understand them profoundly, it is honest questions about these subjects that send the conversation deep. We seek to understand by asking questions and having conversations that matter, and, as I have earlier suggested, when we do, it is understanding that comes to us. These are holy conversations because the Holy Spirit is always present, working through us, in us, and in others, too.

## A FINAL THOUGHT

In this chapter (in fact, in the entire second half of this book), I have tried to make the case that God keeps coming and coming and coming to us. It is God at the center, not us. We are the branches, not the vine (John 15:5). When Jesus told his disciples that he was about to leave them, he comforted them with these words: "And I will ask the Father, and he will give you another advocate to help you and be with you forever—the Spirit of truth. . . . I will not leave you as orphans; *I will come to you*" (John 14:15–18, italics mine).

There it is again—I will come to you. When we pray that we may seek to understand others more than to be understood, we are inviting the Holy Spirit to come. It is a prayer with a foregone conclusion. Thanks be to God.

## QUESTIONS FOR REFLECTION AND DISCUSSION

1. Why is it so easy to talk and so hard to listen? Have you been taught to be a good listener? How might you improve your listening skills?

2. Why is sharing what we know so tempting? What is the payoff when we do?

3. Do you have someone in your life who truly understands you? What makes this relationship so special, so important?

4. From your own life, can you share an example of God coming and coming and coming to you?

5. Which of the three spiritual invitations or desires is most compelling in your life right now—to go deep, to be known, or to find your way home? How would you describe this invitation?

The Prayer of St. Francis
*Lord, make me an instrument of your peace.*
*Where there is hatred, let me sow love;*
*Where there is injury, pardon;*
*Where there is doubt, faith;*
*Where there is despair, hope;*
*Where there is darkness, light;*
*Where there is sadness, joy.*
*O Divine Master,*
*Grant that I may not so much seek*
*To be consoled as to console;*
*To be understood as to understand;*

# 9

## Seeking to Love

### *The Practice of Humility*

Love is patient, love is kind. It does not envy, it does not boast, it is not proud. It does not dishonor others, it is not self-seeking, it is not easily angered, it keeps no record of wrongs. Love does not delight in evil but rejoices in the truth. It always protects, always trusts, always hopes, always perseveres. Love never fails.

—1 CORINTHIANS 13:4–8A

### INTRODUCTION

The apostle Paul, the writer of 1 Cor 13, puts it right out there and sets the bar high, way too high for me most days. You may be feeling much the same way. We desire to join St. Francis in praying to seek to love others more than to be loved ourselves, but how in the world can we do this? How can we live our lives patiently and kindly, not envious, not boastful, not proud? Lives that are not easily angered, self-seeking, or dishonoring of others? Lives that keep no record of wrongs and do not delight in evil but rejoice in the truth? And to top it off, lives that always protect, trust, hope, and persevere—and never fail each other? Impossible, you think, and I think you are right.

I have come to believe that the love Paul is speaking of here is from another world, or more precisely from another kingdom. We can spend our entire lives trying to meet this standard of love. I believe it is a call to live a holy life, to be holy. If we're lucky we would begin to approach this standard of love for others just on this side of the grave—or maybe on the other. It is a quest of a lifetime, and it will take a lifetime.

And when we pray "your kingdom come, your will be done on earth as it is in heaven" as Jesus taught us (Matt 6:10), we are praying to live out a love for others that is the currency of the kingdom of God. We pray for God's kingdom to come on earth, here and now, as it is in heaven, and when we do, we are expressing a profound spiritual insight that loving others as we love ourselves is not just possible, it is a sacred obligation. It is the practice of this sacred obligation, this call to live a holy life full of love, that we will examine in this chapter. Hopefully, we'll end with several concrete steps that we can take to start us on this journey of love, and I'll offer a perspective on what I believe that God expects of us as we do.

## Seeking To Be Loved

Let me start with the obvious—there is nothing wrong with wanting to be loved, even seeking to be loved. We all desire to be embraced and accepted for who we are. We want to know that we are not alone in this world, and love is critical for mature living and healthy growth. We all want that. We are hardwired to pursue it.

However, seeking to be loved can have a dark side, too. Let me mention three ways that seeking to be loved can go sideways or, as my father was fond of saying, will take you down a very bad road. First, seeking to be loved can turn us into performers. That is, we can so desire the attention of someone (or some group) that we end up seeking the spotlight, demanding the spotlight even, looking for ways to be seen that can prove to be unhealthy. We'll do anything and everything to gain attention, hoping that being seen and being loved are the same thing. Sadly, they are not, and it often has the opposite effect on the ones we are seeking—we turn people off and they avoid us like the plague. We end up performing with an empty heart to an empty house.

Second, while we all want others to approve of us, this desire can turn ugly when our need for approval becomes all-encompassing, the only thing that matters. We end up doing all kinds of unhealthy things to get it. We start out dressing and acting in ways that we think will bring acceptance, but we end up not thinking for ourselves at all. We become slaves to what others think or how they act or what they believe. For a misguided sense of approval, we surrender our agency, our ethics, our bodies, even our beliefs. This is a very bad road with no outlet or easy turnaround.

A third avenue of unhealthy love-seeking is inappropriate control. Of course, there are appropriate ways to express love by exercising control, like when parents watch over their young children, correcting them, guiding them, insisting on certain behaviors while disallowing others, and stepping in if necessary. This is the way children learn and develop. However, in a mature relationship, seeking to be loved takes a very bad turn when love must be demonstrated by doing or not doing what others deem appropriate or expect. When it is a case of "If you really love me, you'll . . ." or "You don't really love me if you won't . . . ," submitting to another's control is no way to love or be loved, and controlling another person in the name of love will dry up that relationship like an old leaf.

You may be wondering why I wanted us to think about trying to find love in all the wrong places in a book about putting the Prayer of St. Francis into practice. Good question. I believe that there is a spiritual parallel to the three relational distortions discussed above. It has to do with our relationship with God, who keeps coming and coming to us, even after us, yet we can easily get the roles reversed and start believing and acting like we must find and earn God's love. We seek the spotlight in church to perform on the worship team or work in the nursery or give the announcements, hoping to gain God's attention. We behave in certain ways and believe in certain things to gain God's approval, and some of us live out our lives in fear that if we slip up or make a mistake or stray an inch from the Perfect Plan for our lives, God will not love us anymore. Such beliefs and behaviors can dry up our relationship with God like an old leaf, too.

The good news is that we don't have to do anything to gain God's attention or approval. There is nothing that we can do to make God stop loving us—nothing. It isn't we who must find our way to God; it is God who has been, is, and will keep on finding a way to us. It's hard to understand that it isn't about us and what we must do, it is about God and what God has already done and continues to do. God keeps coming and coming and coming. This is a love relationship without a dead end.

When the Prayer of St. Francis was written many years ago, perhaps the author had some of these spiritual love-seeking detours in mind; perhaps he didn't. I really don't know. But I do know that seeking love appropriately can be challenging for many of us, and accepting and embracing others as they are can be even more so. Let's see how we can approach loving others with grace and good sense as we look at what the apostle Paul has to say to all of us about the very essence of love. I think it will be familiar to most of us.

## Seeking to Love

We have been looking for spiritual practices that will help us console (to see others, chapter 7), understand (to hear others in speech, chapter 8), and love (to accept and embrace others, chapter 9), even when we may be in deep need of the same ourselves. We acknowledged that it is difficult to practice seeing others when it feels like no one is watching over us or out for us. It is difficult to practice hearing others into speech when it seems that no one is listening to us. And let's face it, it is especially hard to accept and embrace others when it seems that the whole world has pushed us away or is so divided into camps that everyone is talking but no one is willing to listen! How do we love in such a context, especially when such a description describes our own church to a T?

Let's begin with the wisdom of St. Paul. He was writing to the church in Corinth, and it was in a big mess and asked Paul for help. He responded with the call to love each other deeply, and the first two virtues he named were patience and kindness (1 Cor 13:4a). Honestly, I guess he could have picked some less-challenging virtues like charity or moderation, and sometimes I wish he had, but he didn't, and with good reason. I think he knew that patience and kindness are at the very heart of the gospel, central to what it takes to truly love one other—to accept and embrace our neighbors for who they are and what they are and not for who and what we want them to be. The good news is that as far as God is concerned, the same goes for us, too. If God is anything, God is patient.

### Love Is Patient

It's difficult to understand God's timing, let alone predict it. When we look back, it is often easy to see God's fingerprints all over our lives, but not so when we look to the future or when we look around for a clue—any clue. What is clear to me is that our God is the God of the Patient Wait. You can turn to almost any place in the Bible, and there you will find God waiting patiently for some thing or another, and humans impatiently waiting and wondering if they have been abandoned. God took six days to create our world. I suppose God could have done so with a wink of an eye and a few magic words, but that didn't happen. And after six days, God rested, although I'm sure there were many other tasks to attend to (Gen 1:1—2:3). God was (and is) a patient creator.

God patiently waited until there was only one righteous family left on earth before unleashing the skies that led to the great flood and then promised never to do it again (Gen 6–9). And God willingly negotiated with Abraham on behalf of Sodom if he could find fifty righteous men—no, forty-five, no forty, thirty-five, thirty, twenty-five, twenty, fifteen, then ten. In the end, Abraham could not find even ten, but I can't help wondering if God would have been willing to patiently negotiate even further (Gen 18:16–33). Obviously, he was in no hurry to destroy that city. We can all be thankful for such mercy.

And God waited patiently for Abraham's grandson Jacob to return home after scheming and fleeing and cutting corners most of his life, and when he did, God gave him a blessing and a new name (Gen 32:22–32). I'll bet that most of us could use a blessing and a new name right about now, too.

The list goes on and on—years in denial, years in bondage in Egypt, years wandering in the desert (often of their own making), years in exile (more than once), years with an erratic king, years with self-absorbed kings, years under siege, and years waiting for the messiah to come, to name just a few. Of course, there were some good years, too, but even then, there was a sense of waiting—that something needed to come and was coming, but it was coming in God's own time, not theirs.

And speaking of God's own timing, we often think of the apostle Paul's Damascus Road experience as three days that transformed Paul's vision and immediately catapulted him on to his missionary journeys. Surely, that experience did change Paul, but there is much more to the story. After a visit from Jesus on the way to Damascus (Acts 9), Paul left and headed south into the Arabian Desert on a pilgrimage, tracing the route taken by one of his heroes, Elijah (1 Kgs 19). After a time, perhaps as much as three years later, he returned to Jerusalem and presented himself to Peter and James, the leaders of the budding but oppressed group of Christ followers. After very brief preaching stints in several local synagogues, Paul was escorted down to Caesarea and put on a boat back to Tarsus, his hometown. He stayed in Tarsus for almost a decade before Barnabas showed up and accompanied him to Antioch, where Paul began his missionary efforts in earnest (Acts 9–11). Even after one of the most life-changing encounters with Jesus ever recorded, Paul had to patiently wait and prepare for his public ministry. God is the God of the Patient Wait—for everyone, even apostles.

Perhaps the best illustration of God's loving patience can be seen in the parable of the prodigal son (Luke 15:11–32). The impetuous younger brother did not want to wait for his inheritance, and even though the father knew that it would be a disaster, he gave his son his share, which he immediately went out and squandered, finally ending up with a job tending and eating with the pigs—not the destination he had envisioned and certainly

not an occupation for any self-respecting Jew. And what was the father doing during all this time? He was patiently waiting for any sign of his son's
silhouette on the horizon, for *any* sign that he wanted to come home, and
as soon as he caught a tiny glimpse of movement a long way away, he took
off at a dead sprint to welcome him home and throw a party in his honor.

There is plenty of good news in this parable for all of us, because we
are prodigals, too, impatient and bull-headed, thinking we know better and
wanting what we want right now! Repeatedly, God has proven to be loving
enough to give us freedom, even when we didn't know where we were going
or what we were going to do when we got there, and patient enough to wait
until we made even the slightest glance toward home. When we did, grace
came running and the celebrations began, which was far more than any of
us ever imagined or deserved. I pray that we will all practice that kind of
patience with each other, loving our neighbors as God has loved us. When
we do, we honor the God of the Patient Wait.

## Love Is Kind

There's no doubt that patience and kindness are a powerful duo. One
strengthens the other. It seems to me that patience is something we can
decide to practice. It is an attitudinal change, although there are certainly
spiritual and relational aspects to it. Kindness, on the other hand, comes
from deep within our spirits. It is the most powerful virtue we can practice,
and many other virtues cannot be summoned without it. Without kindness,
how can we practice compassion, magnanimity, and humility? I don't think
we can.

And I don't think that we can just decide one day to be kind. Such
decisions will only last until the morning coffee break. Kindness is a much
deeper spiritual practice, and it takes time and holy work. Some of us, it
seems, are just kinder—whether by nature or nurture. The good news is,
however, that while we can't just decide to be kind, we can all decide to
be kinder, and it is a cumulative practice. The more we practice it for the
benefit of others, the more it shapes and forms us. I believe that it is the Holy
Spirit working in us.

When I think about the practice of loving kindness, my mother comes
immediately to mind. She was simply the kindest person I have ever known,
and I hope that some of her kindness and acceptance of others has rubbed
off on me. She simply loved and accepted everyone for who they were, everyone. She made no judgments about anyone. They were all welcome in
her home.

I remember one Thanksgiving when my mother learned that one of our relatives would be alone for Thanksgiving. She had a successful professional practice in a neighboring town, but because she was gay and living with her partner, her very religious family would have nothing to do with her. She was not welcome in their home, especially over the holidays. It was more than my mother could stand. I remember watching and listening to my mother as she called our relative and invited her for Thanksgiving dinner—and she was to bring her partner, too. We were all, she said, anxious to meet her. When the couple arrived, carrying a pie and acting a bit nervous, my mother walked between them, gave them both a big hug, a long hug, and told them that she was so glad that they came. I'll never forget the warm smiles all-around. I determined that day that *that* was the kind of person I wanted to be—showing love by embracing and accepting others on the spot, all the time, no questions asked. When St. Paul wrote that love is kind, I think that he was saying much the same thing.

## SCRIPTURE

I have quoted from Scripture throughout this chapter, so I don't feel the need to highlight any more here. Suffice it to say, however, that when we seek to love others, it is a spiritual challenge to embrace and accept others for who they are, where they are, as they are. This is an expression of the love of God, who keeps coming and coming and coming to us, accepting us for who we are, where we are, as we are. And I am challenged when I see the entire arc of the biblical narrative move from exclusion to inclusion. I pray that as we practice the Prayer of St. Francis, the same arc will be evident in our lives, too.

## PRACTICING THE PRAYER OF ST. FRANCIS

St. Paul tells us that at the heart of love is patience and kindness. I think he's spot on, and we have looked at some ways to put patience and kindness into practice. Let's take another step and look now at some very practical ways to practice our prayer to love others. Here are three simple ways to practice love in our own neighborhoods and church fellowships—compassion, openness, and trust.

## Compassion

First, we can practice compassion by seeing others in need, listening others into speech, and embracing and accepting others for who they are, things we have discussed throughout Part II of this book. I suggest that we book-end our days. By this I mean that we start each day with intention and end each day with reflection. As we start each day, we pray for divine assistance to see, hear, and embrace others. It's that simple, and that hard, especially in a culture that keeps telling us that we should look out for number one and that we're the only one who really matters. All the others, especially those who see things differently or look differently, are on their own. As we go about our business, we seek to make God's kingdom our priority and let it encompass our entire day.

And at the end of the day, we pray for insight and do some honest reflecting on how the day went for us—where we were sensitive to others and where we lost our way. It is a daily struggle, but over time with resolve and the help of the Holy Spirit, we can develop spiritual eyes to see and ears to hear, what I have come to believe are at the very heart of loving God and neighbor.

## Openness

Another way to show love for others is to share our own struggles, doubts, and fears. We live in a society that is all too eager to dispense advice ("Do you know what you should do?!") and far too reticent to be honest with each other. We live our lives as if we were on Facebook, always sporting a smile and only posting our best shots, despite how rotten things may be at the time. If we depend on Facebook to see how others are doing, I guarantee you that we will come away thinking that everyone else is living in Disney-land and our lives are as boring as hell. It just isn't reality, and masquerading that way is no way to love anyone.

When listening to someone who is sharing their struggles, doubts, and fears, perhaps the most loving and healing thing we can say is "me, too." Not much else needs to be said.

## Trust

A third way to practice loving others is to understand what we can do for others and what work is above our pay grade. We can take a cue from John the Baptist. The Jewish leaders in Jerusalem sent out priests and Levites to ask him who he was. "Are you Elijah?" they asked. No. "Are you the Prophet?" No, again. "Well, are you the Messiah, then?" No. I am simply a voice of one calling in the wilderness (John 1:19–23). Clearly, John knew his calling and who he was. He also knew who he wasn't. He wasn't the messiah, and neither are we. Part of loving others is to trust God to do the heavy lifting.

In *Eternal Seasons*, Henri Nouwen suggests that the word "patience" means the willingness to stay where we are and live the situation out to the full in the belief that something hidden there will manifest itself to us.[1] I think we can substitute the word "trust" for "patience" and come away with much the same meaning. Trusting in God's timing and the work of the Holy Spirit is a spiritual practice that will change us in ways known and unknown. Thanks be to God!

## A FINAL THOUGHT

Patience and kindness are at the heart of love, Paul tells us. He's right, of course, and I can't help but believe that he would insist that we are to be patient and kind with ourselves, too.

## QUESTIONS FOR REFLECTION AND DISCUSSION

1. Have you seen or experienced a time when seeking to be loved turned out to be a bad road for someone, maybe even yourself? Explain.

2. In this chapter, love is described as the currency of the kingdom of God. Do you agree or disagree? Why or why not?

3. Do you believe that patience and kindness are at the very heart of love as described by St. Paul?

4. Which spiritual discipline seems to be the most difficult for you to consistently practice: compassion, openness, or trust? Why?

5. Why do you think is it easy for so many of us to be patient and kind with others but hard on ourselves? How might we change the equation?

The Prayer of St. Francis
*Lord, make me an instrument of your peace.*
*Where there is hatred, let me sow love;*
*Where there is injury, pardon;*
*Where there is doubt, faith;*

1. Nouwen, *Eternal Seasons*, 38.

*Where there is despair, hope;*
*Where there is darkness, light;*
*Where there is sadness, joy.*
*O Divine Master,*
*Grant that I may not so much seek*
*To be consoled as to console;*
*To be understood as to understand;*
*To be loved as to love.*

# PART III

## Seeing the Full Circle of Grace

THERE ARE MANY THINGS in life that cannot be understood at the time but can only be fully understood when looking backward, sometimes over an entire lifetime. I always smile when I hear a young couple exchange their wedding vows—for better, for worse, for richer, for poorer, in sickness and in health . . . Now please hear me. I am not for one second wanting to diminish the sincerity of those vows. I don't smile because I think that they are being dishonest or insincere. Not at all. I know that their vows are deeply felt and the intentions are real, but I smile nonetheless because I can't help from musing: they really don't have a clue about what they're getting into or what things will come their way. They are making sweeping promises full of hope and grace to each other about life together with a totally unknown future. It is optimism at its best, and I love it!

And I guess that's why I love to hear couples who are celebrating their fiftieth wedding anniversary reflect on their life together. It usually goes something like this: "Well, it hasn't always been easy, and who could have guessed where we would be or what we would be doing right now, but I wouldn't trade the journey together for anything, not anything. God is faithful!" Looking back, they see their tender promises full of grace and hope come full circle.

In this final part of the Prayer of St. Francis, the writer looks back and sees things come full circle, too—in giving, we receive, in pardoning, we are pardoned, and in dying, we are born to eternal life. These are not empty promises or hopeful statements made at the start of one's spiritual journey but the observations of one who looks back and sees God's fingerprints all

over their life. We will take these last three chapters to explore the richness
of seeing grace come full circle and to point out a theological pitfall or two
along the way.

# 10

# Seeing Full Circle

*Blessings Come in the Giving*

No one has ever become poor by giving.

—ANNE FRANK

## INTRODUCTION

"Each of you should give what you have decided in your heart to give, not reluctantly or under compulsion, for God loves a cheerful giver" (2 Cor 9:7). According to Paul, it is the heart, not the head, that guides our giving. Decide in your heart, he tells the church in Corinth, then give—not with reluctance or under duress, but with a spirit of giving.

It is the spirit of giving that we will explore in this chapter, and as we shall see, this spirit can be easily turned on its head. And when it is, it can only lead to what can be described as misguided and self-absorbed theology.

### Quid Pro Quo

In Latin, "quid pro quo" literally means "what for what" or "something for something." Many see quid pro quo as part of the human condition, a natural human instinct that getting something in return for what we do for others is the name of the game. It could be attention, appreciation, status, affection, money, friendship, or the assurance that someone will have our back if we need a favor someday, sort of an insurance policy against being left out on a limb all by ourselves.

Quid pro quo theology is the belief that God operates in much the same way. God wants something for something, too. God wants our faith expressed by what we give to the church, and what God gives back is prosperity and material success. It is at the heart of the prosperity gospel, the belief that when we give to God (usually our money), God will pay us back in spades. Our faith in God translates into material and financial success. In fact, it is the evidence of the power of our faith. We put a little skin in the game, and it pays off for us. What a good deal! And in an upwardly mobile, first-world economy, it works for some. The testimonies roll in: "I started tithing and my income suddenly increased to cover all my bills." "I gave my last $100 to the church, and I received a check in the mail double that amount the next week." "When I started to attend my church and giving regularly, I received a promotion at work with a new car."

Of course, there can be some truth in some of these testimonies. For most of us, our incomes will increase over time. We do receive promotions at work, and most of us are financially better off today than we were five years ago. For that, we can be thankful, but to view any type of financial or material success that we may experience as a quid pro quo payment from a God who first demands something from us, some spiritual skin in the game, simply reduces the God of the universe to some kind of financial wheeler-dealer. Of course, we never hear any testimonies from those who give generously and receive nothing in return (they must lack faith) or from those in third-world economies where God does not appear to be so generous. Honestly, quid pro quo is misguided theology, and sadly, it is seductive, often preying on the misfortunate, the marginalized, the poor, and the desperate. They are drawn to the promise of prosperity, and they pay a huge price when they lose not only their resources but their faith and hope in God as well. We don't hear about these causalities.

We do hear from the successful, however. Their conspicuous consumption is evident to all, and it is a sign, so we are told—and they believe—that God is pleased with them and blesses them with financial and material success. Having and flaunting a lot of stuff becomes a spiritual act, a sign of right belief, and we regularly invite them up front to talk to the rest of us about having more faith. But Jesus said that his kingdom was not of this world; it was from another place (John 18:36). I don't believe that quid pro quo theology has even a glimpse of the kingdom that Jesus was referring to—not at all.

But let's be honest. While I trust that most of us do not believe in the God of the prosperity gospel, most of us most of the time do look for some type of payoff in return when we give. It might be attention, approval, prestige, affection, or status. If we send a gift, we look for a thank-you note or a call, and if it doesn't come, we are quick to judge the recipient as selfish or self-centered. We take a family a meal, hear nothing in return, and make a mental note that that won't happen again. "Happen once, shame on you; happen twice, shame on me!" We work around the church and fume when the work goes unrecognized and unrewarded. We make a financial donation, and we expect to receive some attention from the pastor or the president of the local college. Deep down, we all want to be known as humble *and* generous. Those are wonderful virtues to cultivate, but when the emphasis shifts from being humble and generous to *being known* as humble and generous, the bloom is off the rose.

Yet, the writer of the Prayer of St. Francis, looking back on a lifetime of faithful service, sees that it is in giving that we receive. What is this spirit of giving and what do we receive in return when we give? In the following sections, we'll look first at what we receive when we give before turning to Scripture to examine some spiritual aspects of a giving spirit.

## What Do We Receive When We Give?

What do we receive when we give? On one level, nothing, nothing at all. The spiritual ideal is to give freely, humbly, and generously, without any thought of something for something. When we expect to get something in return, it is not humble giving. Rather, it is good old quid pro quo at work, all too human and as old as the hills, but not the kind of receiving the Prayer of St. Francis is referring to.

This prayer refers to the spiritual blessing we receive when we look back at our lives with the knowledge that we did the best we could to share what we had, at least most of the time. It is in the looking back that contentment, joy, and thankfulness come to us. We don't manufacture it. It is a gift from the God who has always been good to us. When we've had opportunities to emulate God's character and we've followed through with grace, generosity, and humility, we don't become instant saints. But it does give us memory. How it all works, I honestly don't know, but I do know this: at the end of the day, mystery and memory are two of the best companions we will ever have as we journey home.

## SCRIPTURE

The Spirit of Giving, selfless giving, is at the heart of the gospel, but it isn't easy to do. Time and time again, Scripture points out problems that we bring upon ourselves by our love of money, our love of possessions, and our craving for the attention and status we gain from them in one form or another—the Spirit of Having. It is the engine, shame, and curse of first-world life.

To be clear, it isn't that money is the root of all evil. Having money does not make you a bad person, but as Paul cautioned his young charge Timothy, "The love of money is a root of all kinds of evil. Some people, eager for money, have wandered from the faith and pierced themselves with many griefs" (1 Tim 6:10). It is a caution we should all take seriously.

I want to briefly highlight just two of the problems that can accompany the Spirit of Having. First, Jesus was quite clear that making yourself the center of attention is not the way to give: "So when you give to the needy, do not announce it with trumpets, as the hypocrites do in the synagogues and on the streets, to be honored by others" (Matt 6:2a). Leave the trumpets at home and give generously without the fanfare.

Jesus felt much the same way about those who made a big spectacle of their giving, even at the temple, perhaps especially at the temple: "Jesus sat down opposite the place where the offerings were put and watched the crowd putting their money into the temple treasury. Many rich people threw in large amounts" (Mark 12:41), making sure that everyone saw how much they gave. That didn't sit well with Jesus. Perhaps that is one reason why he pointed out the poor widow who came and gave only two very small cooper coins, telling his disciples that she gave more than all the others (Mark 12:42–44). Obviously, God sees things differently than we do and understands their significance differently, too.

A second problem that comes with the Spirit of Having is threatening to withhold your giving if you don't get your way or refusing to give at all as a punishment for something you don't like. Honestly, this is a naked misuse of giving power, and it happens in the church more than I care to admit. It is contrary to the Spirit of Giving: selfless, humble, and full of grace. What we give, how we give, and how we use the influence we gain by giving is up to each of us. I think there is guidance in Prov 3:27: "Do not withhold good from those to whom it is due, when it is in your power to act." That's good advice for all of us who desire to practice the Spirit of Giving.

## PRACTICING THE PRAYER OF ST. FRANCIS

Let me suggest four commitments that will shape us as we desire to put the Spirit of Giving into practice. First, *determine to be a giver*. Give regularly, generously, and faithfully. In my personal finance course in college, the professor gave the following advice: "Each month, give away 10 percent of your income, save 10 percent of your income, and live off the other 80 percent. The older you get, the easier it gets. The percentages can be adjusted to meet circumstances, but the principle is clear—live within your means and make giving a priority. As you look back on your life, you'll be glad you did." Since then, I have followed his advice as best I could, and I'm glad I did. It makes the Spirit of Giving a priority, not an afterthought.

Second, when you give, give anonymously if you can and privately with little fanfare if you can't. Don't make a big deal about it, and don't let the recipients do so either, no matter how much they want to focus on your gift—or on you. Such celebrations are seductive and hard on our humility. A simple "thank you" and a smile should be sufficient.

Third, speaking of receiving expressions of appreciation, don't expect that everyone will stop and take the time to appropriately thank you for your generosity, no matter what type of gift you gave or how much it was needed at the time. If you do, you'll be sadly disappointed and disillusioned. Remember, when Jesus stopped and healed ten men who had leprosy, only one returned to thank him, and he was a Samaritan, the story tells us—the outcast among the outcasts (Luke 17:11–19). If Jesus' thank-you rate was 10 percent, can we realistically expect to do any better? If we do, we'll end up with our feelings hurt. Maintaining the Spirit of Giving requires a short memory.

Finally, when we are on the receiving end of the giving, do take time to send a note or personally express appreciation for another's generosity, no matter how small the gesture. Extending appreciation is a spiritual practice that will shape us, too.

## A FINAL THOUGHT

Perspective is everything. When we look back and reflect on our lives and think about our meager attempts to live out the Giving Spirit, we remember God's faithfulness to us no matter what. We begin to see that it *is* in the giving that we receive—joy, contentment, and thanksgiving. That's a divine thank-you note from another Kingdom!

## QUESTIONS FOR REFLECTION AND DISCUSSION

1. Do you agree that quid pro quo is a basic human attitude? Why or why not?

2. Do you think that quid pro quo theology distorts our understanding of God? How?

3. Why do you think the other nine lepers failed to return and offer thanks to Jesus?

4. Do you practice the Spirit of Giving by giving regularly and generously? If not, what might be a good first step in developing this practice?

5. Looking back, in the giving have you received? What did you receive?

The Prayer of St. Francis
*Lord, make me an instrument of your peace.*
*Where there is hatred, let me sow love;*
*Where there is injury, pardon;*
*Where there is doubt, faith;*
*Where there is despair, hope;*
*Where there is darkness, light;*
*Where there is sadness, joy.*
*O Divine Master,*
*Grant that I may not so much seek*
*To be consoled as to console;*
*To be understood as to understand;*
*To be loved as to love.*
*For it is in giving that we receive;*

# 11

## Seeing Full Circle

### *Forgiveness Comes in the Pardoning*

Forgiveness is the final form of love.

—REINHOLD NIEBUHR

### INTRODUCTION

It is in the pardoning that we are pardoned, so declares the Prayer of St. Francis. "Pardon" is a strange word for me; it doesn't quite fit this prayer, at least in English. Whatever the writer originally meant by using "pardon" (the prayer was first published in 1912—in French), "pardon" has lost some of its punch, its power, its challenge. If we bump into someone at the grocery store, we say, "Oh, pardon me," meaning excuse me. Clearly, the writer intended something much deeper than "it is in the excusing that we are excused."

In today's world, a pardon exempts someone from the rightful punishment for a crime. It doesn't mean that the person is innocent, only that they do not have to serve out their full sentence or the terms of punishment apportioned for the crime. Pardons can be conditional, too, and generally do not expunge convictions. It is only the punishment that is shortened. We hear most often of pardons being offered by elected officials, a governor or president, for example. And while there are surely many good reasons for giving pardons, they sometimes smack of political and personal influence. Again, I'm sure the prayer's writer intended something deeper, something more spiritual than having our own punishment shortened when we do the same for others.

Pardon can also mean forgiveness, and that's what we will explore in this chapter; "it is in the forgiving that we are forgiven." That is much more challenging for us, summoning something from deep within. Forgiving someone asks something of us, requires something spiritual from us, summons our best selves, and changes us as it is seriously practiced. But forgiving can be one of the hardest things we will ever be bidden to do, even for Christians, perhaps especially for those who claim Christ. Honestly, there are times when we don't want to forgive. No, we want a pound of flesh. We want to see them get what they deserve. We want to see things come around that go around. We want to see the full sentence served, even though we know that we are called to do otherwise.

Ultimately, forgiving is a conscious, deliberate choice, a decision we make. It is intentional and voluntary, and it is often more of a process or series of steps than a single, direct, isolated decision. And can it take time, lots of time, involving acknowledging and embracing our hurt and anger, deciding to forgive, coming to a place where we can extend forgiveness, and dealing with and learning from our own lingering memories and emotional pain. It isn't simple. It is hard work, spiritual work, but this holy work will shape and form us in honest and humble ways. I have come to believe that working to extend forgiveness to others (and to ourselves) is fundamental to the call to be holy persons. The apostle Peter put it this way: "But just as he who called you is holy, so be holy in all you do; for it is written: 'Be holy, because I am holy'" (1 Pet 1:15–16). And if we know anything about God, we know that God is all about forgiveness.

In this next section, we'll look at how some Christians have understood forgiveness as an obligation for receiving forgiveness themselves. Others see it differently. Even the teachings of Jesus from the Sermon on the Mount can be confusing. Hopefully, I will be able to shed some light on the discussion without adding to the confusion.

## Forgiveness

Which is harder—to forgive or to accept forgiveness? Some Christians believe that the two are directly and proportionally related. That is, we are forgiven only to the extent that we are forgiving, and if we don't forgive, then

God will not forgive us. When a killer entered a one-room Amish school in Nickel Mines, Pennsylvania, on October 2, 2006, dismissed all but ten girls, and then killed five before shooting himself, the Amish families and community quickly gathered to express forgiveness for the killer and his family. For most of the world, their actions seemed utterly crazy, incomprehensible, thinking that they must have been emotionally overwhelmed with grief and acted irrationally. Not so, those gathered told the press. "We *must* forgive, because if we don't, God will not forgive us. Our salvation depends on forgiving others."

I know that this is an extreme example, but how in the world could anyone come to such an understanding of God's grace? It sounds like a quid pro quo arrangement, something for something, grace for grace. Where did this understanding of God come from? As it turns out, the Amish were doing their best to understand and practice the teachings of Jesus, particularly from his Sermon on the Mount (Matt 5–7), and specifically his comments about forgiving that were made to his disciples right after he taught them how to pray, what is now known as the Lord's Prayer: "For if you forgive other people when they sin against you, your heavenly Father will also forgive you. But if you do not forgive others their sins, your Father will not forgive your sins" (Matt 6:14–15). There it is. Indeed, this is a very hard teaching, and for me, a very troubling view of God's mercy and grace. How can this possibly be?

It comes from a literal reading of the Bible and is undergirded by a belief in the inerrancy of Scripture that emerged in the mid-sixteenth century—that the Bible is without error in all its teachings. This view is prevalent today among many Christians. For example, the Moody Bible Institute affirms the verbal and factual inerrancy of the Bible, asserting that the Bible is infallible in all it declares to be true, although, they add, Christians may be fallible in their interpretation of the Bible. Thus, it follows, the need for a Bible institute. Other fellowships declare that the Bible is infallible and inerrant, but only in the original manuscripts (although none of the original manuscripts now exist as far as we know).

I believe the admitted need for interpretation, the lack of original manuscripts, the inconsistency of practice, and other contextual factors should give any Christian pause who sincerely maintains that the Scriptures must be read literally—verse by verse by verse. Can we read all Scripture that way? Honestly, I don't think so, and honestly, I don't think that many of us do.

Let me explain by looking closer at Matt 6:14–15, the verses that many quote to demonstrate that God will only forgive us to the extent that we forgive others—something for something, grace for grace. To begin, Matthew, the second oldest Gospel, was most likely written somewhere between AD 80 and 90, with a possible range of AD 70 to 110. Clearly it wasn't written until long after Jesus' death, so his teachings were passed along orally for several generations. We all know what happens when teachings and sayings are passed along, particularly over eight or nine decades. Exact details are forgotten, or changed, or dropped—others are added.

Some scholars surmise that the parenthetical nature of Matt 6:14–15 and the sudden shift in topic, coming right after the Lord's Prayer, suggest that it was added by a writer at a later date long after Jesus' death to buttress a particular debate position about God's grace during that time. Honestly, we do not really know, and honestly, we do not really know who wrote the Gospel of Matthew in the first place. Its authorship is unknown, its intended audience is unknown, and we do not know what, if anything, has been added or dropped or changed after it was first written and circulated. We just don't know—and that's my point. We don't know, so how can we attempt to read literally a story that has gone through several translations two thousand years later and be certain that it is *exactly* the words that Jesus spoke? I don't think we can.

And if we are honest, I don't think most biblical literalists are uniform literalists. That is, we all pick and choose what scriptures we read and what meaning we ascribe to the verses when we do. For example, many take Matt 6:14–15 literally, but not Matt 18:8–9: "If your hand or your foot causes you to stumble, cut it off and throw it away. It is better for you to enter life maimed or crippled than to have two hands or two feet and be thrown into eternal fire. And if your eye causes you to stumble, gouge it out and throw it away. It is better for you to enter life with one eye than to have two eyes and be thrown into the fire of hell." I simply ask you—how many Christians take these words of Jesus literally and practice them faithfully? None that I know of, and we would probably move to have them committed if they did!

Finally, the idea that God only will forgive us in the exact way and to the exact amount that we have forgiven others paints God as a meticulous bean counter of grace, watching and counting everything we do and don't do and treating us accordingly. That is not the nature of the God who loves each of us more than we can imagine, keeps on coming and coming and coming after us and to us. In the story of the prodigal son, the father ran to his son and almost squeezed the breath out of him before he could get back home. The father didn't make him take a shower and change his clothes before receiving the embrace of his life. That's the God I have come to know.

So, how do we read this passage on forgiving others, or any similar Scriptural passage? We read them seriously, prayerfully, carefully, thoughtfully, and corporately. We read seriously when we affirm the holy nature of Scripture that is full of wisdom, grace, and truth. It has something life-giving to say to us, so we pay attention and read with spiritual interest. We read prayerfully when we invite the Holy Spirit to be our ever-present teacher, to guide us and instruct us as we study and strive to learn to live a holy life each day. We let that still small voice speak to us. We read carefully when we neither dismiss the Bible as having nothing relevant to say to us nor take everything literally as though it was written specifically for us and sent to us in a time capsule. We read thoughtfully when we invite our reading and understanding of Scripture to be informed by reason, tradition, and our own experience. Devoted followers of Jesus have thought seriously and studied the Scriptures for centuries, and God has given all of us a brain. God expects us to use it. We can reflect on what we read in Scripture, what others throughout the ages have thought about the passages we are reading, and what our own experience and reason tell us about the passage and the nature of God. And we read corporately when we invite others to join our study of Scripture. Learning to read, understand, and live out Scripture is a long-term team event, not a lonely marathon with no course map or road markings to follow. We really do need each other.

## The Full Circle of Forgiveness—Receiving and Seeing

If the Prayer of St. Francis is correct that forgiving and forgiveness come full circle like giving and receiving, how does it work, especially when we leave the quid pro quo spiritual understanding of God behind? As we work to forgive others (it is a process that we will outline in the "Practicing" section to come), we are more inclined to accept forgiveness from others. As we do the emotional and spiritual work that goes into forgiving others, we see that others have done the same work as they extend forgiveness to us. It is ours for the seeing. And over time, as we practice giving and receiving forgiveness, we are more apt to forgive ourselves, one of the most difficult things to do for many of us. As it turns out, forgiving ourselves is a spiritual process, too.

The entire forgiveness and forgiving process is kingdom work because we are modeling the very character of God, and when we do, we are shaped and formed in God's likeness. If we truly desire to live a holy life, forgiving and receiving forgiveness is a good place to start. And at the end of the day and at the end of our days, we see that it was in the forgiving that we have received forgiveness. Grace is a spectacular thing. Thanks be to God.

## SCRIPTURE

As it turns out, extending forgiveness is a personal matter, a complicated matter, and a spiritual matter. Not so with keeping the law. That is much easier. You just learn the rules and keep them. It is about our behavior, not about our intent or attitude. Take carrying a Roman soldier's pack, for example. In Jesus' time, the Roman law compelled all Jewish citizens to carry a soldier's pack for a mile immediately upon request, about a thousand paces. They could not refuse without severe punishment, and they didn't. However, as they trudged along under the enormous weight of the pack, they would regularly say under their breath: "Just wait until the messiah comes. We'll see then who carries the packs. We'll just see. Can't wait!"

In his Sermon on the Mount (Matt 5–7), Jesus turned this pack-carrying scenario on its head: "If anyone forces you to go with them one mile, go with them two miles" (Matt 5:41). What? Go an *extra* mile? Are you serious? Yes, that's what Jesus told the crowd. Obviously, when he said that his kingdom was not of this world, but from another place, he really meant it (John 18:36).

Jesus did much the same when Peter asked him how many times he must forgive someone who sins against him. Was it seven times as prescribed by the law? After seven times, of course, you are free to write them off, but I can't help thinking that Peter was hoping for a lesser number, maybe three times, maybe only once. After all, seven means *a lot*! But Jesus told him it is not seven times, but seventy or even seventy times seven (depending on the translation) (Matt 18:21–22). That's not a lot, that's *infinite*. Jesus' meaning is clear. We are to forgive and keep on forgiving and forgiving and forgiving, even losing count of the number of times that forgiveness has been extended. If we're honest, this is just what God has done with us, losing count of the number of times we have been forgiven. We are all sinners saved by grace, of course, and it is rarely a one-time event. That's a good thing for all of us to ponder.

## PRACTICING THE PRAYER OF ST. FRANCIS

Forgiving is a decision within a process, ultimately a spiritual endeavor that changes us even as we strive to love God and neighbor. I include family members as neighbors, too. I think that this is what this line in the prayer is getting at—it is in the forgiving that we are forgiven. In the end, it is each of us who are changed as we forgive others, often a process that comes in stages—lament, envision, journey, and resolution.

## Lament

While forgiving someone for forgetting your birthday may be easy, forgiving someone who has hurt you deeply with unkind words or deliberate actions is not. In most cases, the first step in forgiveness is not some kind of grand cathartic meeting and resolution. Rather, it is to take the time to be honest, to admit that you are hurt, and to acknowledge, embrace, and grieve the personal pain and loss you are experiencing. It is not a silly act of self-absorption, but a healthy and necessary beginning. I grew up in a family that didn't show or share emotions, didn't even admit that we had any! It was always "stiff upper lip time." I had to learn the hard way that when you repress your emotions, your stomach keeps score.

It may seem counterintuitive, but the first step in forgiving someone is to be real with yourself and a few trusted others about what you have experienced and the emotional and relational damage done. It is not only ok to lament what happened to you, it is essential that you do. Go ahead and grieve. You have my permission and my encouragement. It is the first step of a healthy, healing, spiritual journey.

## Envisioning a Possible Future

The second step may seem obvious, but it is not. At some point in the forgiveness process as you acknowledge and deal honestly with your own hurt, you decide that you will forgive someday. It will not be today, and it may not be tomorrow, but you hope and trust that sometime in the future you will be able to forgive. You begin to catch a shadowy glimpse of what restoration might look like, what you hope could someday be. Envisioning a possible future is the second step in forgiveness.

## Journey

Once you decide that forgiveness is possible, someday, the journey begins. It is a spiritual journey, and each journey is different. Be sensitive to the leading of the Holy Spirit and to opportunities that present themselves. It may be a simple cordial word or smile in passing, or you might unexpectedly find yourself together in the same checkout line or the same crew on Serve Day or thrown together at a family funeral. Trust the work and leading of the Holy Spirit. View such opportunities not as a simple coincidence or an irritation or a nightmare but rather as a chance to begin to reestablish a relationship, no matter how small the first steps may be or how many there are. Start the journey as a spiritual practice. Just put one foot in front of the other, and let the Holy Spirit do the heavy lifting.

## Resolution

In a perfect world, the person who has hurt you deeply will come to you, sincerely apologize, and ask for forgiveness, to which you respond with grace. The relationship is cautiously restored, and all is well. Of course, it isn't a perfect world. If such a development does occur, embrace it and give thanks to God.

But what if you never receive an apology? The offending person never apologizes for their behavior, not admitting that they did anything hurtful or not remembering what they did or simply not caring. They have moved on, and you are left behind. What then? You forgive anyway, let go, and move on. It doesn't mean that the scars or hard memories simply vanish, but it does mean that you choose to move on with your eyes upward, your feet forward, and your heart open. In the forgiving, you find that you have been forgiven, too, and you have a deeper understanding and trust of the God who forgives and forgives and forgives because that is what it means to love someone. As Niebuhr put it, *forgiveness is the final form of love.*[1] I think he's right.

After coming to a resolution, no matter how complete or satisfactory, it is good to reflect on the experience, attempting to understand what we have learned from the experience, what God may be attempting to teach us right now, and how we will make our way in the future. I believe the Holy Spirit can use even our most painful experiences as teachable moments as we journey home.

At the end of the day, forgiving has always been a matter of the heart, and we find that forgiveness comes even as we forgive others.

## A FINAL WORD

Our lives are shaped by the stories we tell, the heroes we admire, and the way we treat our neighbors. May our stories, our heroes, and our actions be filled with grace and forgiveness as we imitate the heart of God.

1. Niebuhr, *Irony of American History*, 63.

## QUESTIONS FOR REFLECTION AND DISCUSSION

1. Which is harder for you—to forgive or to ask for forgiveness? Explain.

2. Do you find it difficult to forgive yourself when you have come up short, even though others have forgiven you? Why is it so hard?

3. Do you agree that forgiving is more of a process or journey than a one-off event?

4. Have you forgiven someone even though they didn't ask for forgiveness (and probably never will)? What steps did you take to come to that point of grace and forgiveness?

5. Is it easy for you to let go and move on after difficulties with someone? Why or why not?

The Prayer of St. Francis
*Lord, make me an instrument of your peace.*
*Where there is hatred, let me sow love;*
*Where there is injury, pardon;*
*Where there is doubt, faith;*
*Where there is despair, hope;*
*Where there is darkness, light;*
*Where there is sadness, joy.*
*O Divine Master,*
*Grant that I may not so much seek*
*To be consoled as to console;*
*To be understood as to understand;*
*To be loved as to love.*
*For it is in giving that we receive;*
*It is in pardoning that we are pardoned;*

# 12

## Seeing Full Circle

### *New Life Comes in the Dying*

This resurrection life you received from God is not a timid, grave-tending life. It's adventurously expectant, greeting God with a childlike "What's next, Papa?"

—ROMANS 8:15 (MSG)

### INTRODUCTION

In my writings and daily reading, I use the New International Version (NIV), but sometimes, and this is one of those times, The Message (MSG), written by Eugene Peterson, gets to the heart of the matter better than any other translation or paraphrase: "So don't you see that we don't owe this old do-it-yourself life one red cent. There's nothing in it for us, nothing at all. The best thing to do is give it a decent burial and get on with your new life. God's Spirit beckons. There are things to do and places to go!" (Rom 8:12–14 MSG). Honestly, I couldn't have said it better myself—new life for old!

There are many ways to approach the last phrase in St. Francis's prayer: "It is in the dying that we are born to eternal life." In this chapter, I want us to think about giving our old life a decent burial and getting on with our new lives, as The Message puts it. We'll use the different elements of this paraphrase to do so, but first I want to share a personal story about getting on with a new life. Transitions are hard but necessary for all of us. Thankfully, we don't have to journey alone.

## Passage

When I walked into the office as the new university provost, a fancy title for an academic dean or chief academic officer, I felt that I was at the top of my game. You see, I had served in this capacity at several other institutions over the previous twenty years, and I had a strong record of developing, inspiring, and leading the faculty with a focus on quality, community, and faithful service. The faculty search committee told me that they could tell that I loved my work. I told them that this was my calling, my passion, my ministry.

Soon after my arrival on campus, however, things began to fall apart. While my former relationships with university presidents were that of a close friend, colleague, and partner, it became evident that this would not be the case with my new boss. I was simply a direct report, nothing more—not a partner, not a colleague, not a friend. And as it turned out, I must have been an irritating one at that. In his eyes, I couldn't do anything right. I couldn't figure out what was expected of me, how much detail he wanted me to report to him, or even how I was to relate to him. It was all very confusing.

And early on, I learned that I couldn't trust much of what he told me. When the time came to renew my three-year contract, I received a two-year contract instead, and was told that all senior staff members were receiving two-year contracts that year until their new strategic plans were submitted. Soon thereafter, I found out that the other members of the senior team received the standard three-year contact, and my contract was not changed even after I submitted my revised strategic plan several times. More confusion, but I knew that it wasn't a sign of support.

In the final year of my two-year contract, my boss told me in no uncertain terms that he did not have the same confidence in me that he had in the other members of the senior team, and my next contract would be for only one year. When pressed for an explanation, he wouldn't give one. Knowing that the senior team had already experienced more than its fair share of involuntary turnover, it was clear to me that I was on the hot seat, and it didn't take a mathematician to project that when a contract goes from three years to two years to one year, the next one would be zero. In other words, I'd be out of a job—the one I came to do and felt called to do. About the same time,

I learned that several of my trusted direct reports were working behind my back and going over my head to other senior officers, making important decisions without my knowledge or input that were mine to make. I struggled to make it through each day, praying that I would do my job with grace and dignity, but I came home tired, stressed out, my cup empty. Deep down I knew it was time to act before I received the axe.

In one respect, the easiest thing to do would have been to find another job and move on. I did have a solid track record and many good friends and contacts in higher education, so a change was certainly possible. In fact, I filled out several applications and received some good offers, but in the end, I was reluctant to accept them. Honestly, I didn't want to move again and start over, and my wife was in the middle of a very fine seminary program, a program that I dearly wanted her to finish. Moving on would make that possibility very unlikely. The best option, it seemed to me, was to try to negotiate a transition to some other position in the university and finish my career there. I proposed to my boss that I move to a faculty position. He accepted my proposal, and I was thankful he did. Still, it felt like a public failure, leaving my senior position without accomplishing all that I had set out to do, an embarrassing thud in full view of the entire university community. And I was deeply wounded, too.

As might be expected, my arrival in my new department was met with a mixture of uncertainty, suspicion, concern, and fear. I didn't blame anyone. They had little say about the former provost joining their ranks, and they didn't know if I was a mole, an informant, a rabble-rouser, or just another discarded administrator. Still, they welcomed me, even if cautiously, and I began to prepare to teach—something I hadn't done full-time in over twenty-five years. And for most of the year, the courses would be taught online. As you might expect, this was a steep learning curve for the former provost.

I knew that it would take time to adjust to my new assignment, so I embraced it as a unique learning opportunity. What I didn't expect, however, was that I would become virtually invisible in a matter of minutes. After all, my former position was prominent, powerful, and important (at least I thought so), and I was "in the know" about almost everything that went on at the university. There was a certain status to being the provost, but now I was across campus in exile—in an office about the size of a jail cell with no windows. My email messages dropped from about five hundred each day to less than ten, and the dozens of persons I counted as good friends turned out to be less than five. There were no waiting lines to get in to see me. In fact, no one came to my office at all! Honestly, I was disappointed and embarrassed to step down from my position, a career-ending move in full view of the campus community, but losing my identity was harder still. When someone asked me what I did at the university, I would tell them, "I teach in the doctoral program in the School of Education," but then quickly add, "but I was the provost," as if that would somehow grant me a bit more status and credibility. Looking back, my response was very sad. I started each day by praying, "Oh, God, give me strength to live another day." Clearly, I was in survival mode, trying to fake my way through, despite my pain, embarrassment, and deep sadness.

Each summer, our program begins with a face-to-face summer intensive lasting several weeks. I was assigned to be the co-instructor for the leadership course. Of course, given the developments over the past year, I felt more like a failure than a leader, more of an impostor than an expert. I really doubted that I had anything to offer these bright, eager students. Still, I showed up on Monday with a smile and did my best to be cordial and positive. It took most of my energy to do so. The co-instructor told me that she would be gone the first Friday, so the class would be mine. I said, "Great!" but I was really feeling a bit queasy, hoping that I would not fall flat on my face.

I worked all week to prepare for Friday, and the morning hours went by quickly. I had twice as much material than I could possibly cover. The students were intent and appreciative as I offered them some ways to think about leadership that could be used in their own work settings. I must admit that I was feeling good about the class and about myself when I packed up to leave for lunch—I was going to be alright. That morning, my wife baked a Bundt cake for the class, which of course was met with genuine appreciation. I brought the cake in a cake carrier, the kind with a glass dome that sits on top of a cake stand, but this version didn't have any grooves to hold the dome in place. On the way to school, I used some tape to secure the dome in place, but I forgot to tape the dome before I left class. You can probably guess what happened next. In a crowded hallway, right outside the lunchroom where all the students and faculty were gathered, the glass cake dome slid off the stand, hit the floor with a loud crash, and shattered into a million pieces. Of course, I was embarrassed, even though several students and staff members quickly jumped in to help clean up the mess, but I felt something much deeper, something begging to be acknowledged. It hit me as I stood there surveying the broken mess that it wasn't just the cake dome that was on the floor smashed to pieces—my career, my identity, and my spirit were smashed into a million pieces, too. I had no idea how to clean up that mess.

I didn't have much of an appetite, so I took a walk before returning for the afternoon class. I could not have been gone more than forty-five minutes, but when I opened my office door, there it was on my desk. A big white box with a note on top that simply read: *From your friends in the 2013 Cohort.*

Inside was a new glass cake plate dome. I just stood there with tears running down my cheeks. What a moment of healing and grace. A student told me later that they didn't want me to go home to my wife without a cake plate dome. And as it turns out, I went home with something else, too. I had a new identity, a new career, and my spirit was starting to mend. After that day, when I was asked what I did at the university, I would proudly say, "I'm a professor, and I love what I do—and even more, I love my students." It was a passage.[1]

When I retired five years later, it was clear that my teaching years were some of the very best of my entire academic career.

## New Life for Old

Transitions are often difficult, even when they are desired, and almost certainly painful when they are not. Whether it is a loss of a job, a friendship, a home, or a church, or dealing with a divorce or a retirement or a debilitating illness, each transition brings on its own unique season of loss, and it takes time to deal with the fatigue and heal from the feelings of shame, guilt, and disappointment that linger. So, how do we get on with the new? In what follows, we'll see that it is more of a process than a single, independent decision, and it can be a formative communal passage. We need not journey alone.

### The Spirit of God Beckons

When we start the process of trading an old life for a new one, it is important to recognize that God is with us, no matter who or what caused this passage. And especially if it was our own selfish actions and poor decisions that landed us in a bad place, God is already there, wherever there is, at work, reminding us, calling us, beckoning us to a journey to new life. It isn't just that we don't have to do this on our own, in our own strength, but that God has something in mind for us—to flourish, to go deep, and to become more like Jesus. The Spirit of God beckons us to new life and is prepared to guide us every step of the way. It isn't an aimless journey without hope or direction.

### Give Your Old Life a Decent Burial

I love walking a labyrinth, any labyrinth, but especially one that is modeled after the labyrinth on the floor of the Chartres Cathedral. For some reason, it fits my stride and my spirit. One such labyrinth can be found at a church

1. Some of this story first appeared in Allen, *For Today*, 120–23. Used by permission.

not far from my home, and I've walked it many times. In the Middle Ages, those who could not manage a pilgrimage to Jerusalem would walk a labyrinth instead. I'm one of those pilgrims.

There is only one way in and one way out. As you make your way slowly to the center of the labyrinth, you reflect on your life and the burdens you are carrying. When you reach the center, representing the cross of Jesus, you leave your burdens, pain, and disappointments there and begin the journey back to the finish, looking forward to a fresh start. It is a wonderful spiritual practice.

As I approached retirement, I walked the labyrinth, carrying my fears and anxieties about retirement with me. As I left them at the cross, I felt the Spirit of God beckon me, "Follow me and write. You now have all the time you need. Get on with it!" I gave my former career a decent burial and didn't look back.

Of course, not all of us will hear the Spirit of God beckon us in such direct terms, but God does beckon us to new life—all of us. We begin by acknowledging that God is present with us and for us, and we continue by giving our old life a decent burial. At funerals, it is appropriate to grieve the loss. So, too, with transitions. Often, symbolic acts like walking a labyrinth, crossing a bridge, taking a trip, throwing something away, removing a decal from your car, or reorganizing your routine or your office help to make the burial seem more concrete. However we do so, we want to signal that we know that God is with us, the source of our hope, and we are ready for a new journey. *"It's adventurously expectant, greeting God with a childlike 'What's next, Papa?'"* Yes, what's next, indeed!

## Get On With Your New Life

Get on with your new life. It sounds so easy, but for most of us, it simply isn't, because the pain and disappointment hang on like a cat on the end of a tree branch—frozen in place, nowhere to climb and afraid to let go. We've all been there. Moving forward does not mean that we ignore or deny the pain and disappointment we feel. Instead, we acknowledge it and embrace it. We lament what we feel and grieve what might have been. We try to understand what happened to us and what God might be teaching us from the experience.

At the funeral for our old life, we come and pay our respects, but we do not despair. As we leave, we look to the future with hope, no matter how tentatively, acknowledging that the God of the Universe beckons us to new life. Ahead of us are things for us to do, places for us to go, and people for us to love. It is new life—full of promise, full of hope, full of mystery. *"What's next, Papa?"* We can only imagine as we take our first timid steps, but as our new adventure begins, we trade old life for new.

## SCRIPTURE

When the prophet Isaiah conveyed a message from the Lord, Israel was in Babylonian exile. And after seventy years, there was plenty of reason for grief, anger, cynicism, and despair, but the message was full of hope for a new life: "Forget the former things; do not dwell on the past. See, I am doing a new thing! Now it springs up; do you not perceive it?" (Isa 43:18–19). Don't dwell on the past, but look instead for a new thing. God is present and at work among us. Are we watching? Can we see it? Can we believe it?

I think we've all been in exile of one kind or another at one time or another, perhaps even now. What wonderful words for exiles: "I am doing a new thing. Can you see it?" But living in exile can be seriously exhausting. It drains the spirit. We want to soar like an eagle, run and not be weary, walk and not faint, but there's no wind in our sails, no gas in the tank. Fortunately, we do not soar or run or even walk on our own strength. It is a gift from God. Isaiah puts it this way: "He gives strength to the weary and increases the power of the weak. Even youths grow tired and weary, and young men stumble and fall; but those who hope in the Lord will renew their strength. They will soar on wings like eagles; they will run and not grow weary, they will walk and not be faint" (Isa 40:29–31). That sounds like new life to me.

As it turns out, hope, newfound strength, and renewal are all gifts from a loving God. We do not generate them. In fact, we cannot generate them. They are given to us. Our job is to recognize them, accept them with thanksgiving, and go to work. New life for old.

## PRACTICING THE PRAYER OF ST. FRANCIS

I've offered some practical ways to practice trading an old life for a new one, so I'll do my best to summarize here without being too repetitive.

### Plan a Memorial Service

I don't mean for us to reserve a space and time in a local church for a memorial service as we would to remember and honor a loved one who has passed away. I don't mean *that* kind of memorial service, but I do mean to suggest that we set aside some time, perhaps in the company of a few good friends and loved ones, perhaps by yourself, to remember and give honor to that which has been lost. It is ok to remember that good things happened, friendships were deepened, and God was honored in that which was lost. Although we feel a deep sense of loss as we retire or move on or start over, it is ok, even necessary, to remember that there were good times. A mixture of smiles and tears are always welcome at a memorial service.

## Ask What's Next

I trust that I've made it clear throughout this chapter that our hope is in the Lord and that God has something in mind for each of us. Our task is to stop, look, listen, and discern—and wait. This is no easy task, but necessary. At the start of each day, set aside some time for serious listening, and as you go through each day, keep your spiritual eyes and ears open. You'll be amazed by the opportunities for ministry you see and hear—in due time.

## Walk with Wise Friends

I believe that God often calls to us, but like the young Samuel, we don't recognize the voice or see the opportunities that are right in front of us. We need the wisdom of an Eli, one who has "been there and done that" (1 Sam 3:1–10). It is important to have wise, mature persons in our lives. They can often discern the voices we hear and point us in the right direction or keep us from heading into a swamp of one kind or another.

I particularly love 1 Sam 3:11, "And the Lord said to Samuel: 'See, I am about to do something in Israel that will make the ears of everyone who hears about it tingle.'" My prayer for each of us is that the Lord will do something in our lives that will make the ears of everyone who hears about it tingle—and in the process, it is God who will be honored, both through our mountaintop experiences and even more so through our dark and painful valleys. We are never alone.

## A FINAL WORD

When we see grace come full circle, it catches us by surprise. We stand in amazement. I think God just smiles and asks, "What did you expect? It's what I do. New life for old!"

## QUESTIONS FOR REFLECTION AND DISCUSSION

1. Why do you think that life transitions are so difficult and painful for many of us?

2. Do you believe that God beckons us to new life, that God has something in mind for each of us, even during our failures or in their aftermath? Explain.

3. How would you approach planning a memorial service for some aspect of your life that you are grieving? What would be the next steps? What is keeping you from starting this journey right now?

4. What specific practices could you undertake to discern God's voice and direction?

5. Do you have an Eli in your life, someone with wisdom and understanding, someone you trust to help you discern the voice of the Holy One? If not, where might you find such a person, and could you be such a person for someone else?

The Prayer of St. Francis
*Lord, make me an instrument of your peace.*
*Where there is hatred, let me sow love;*
*Where there is injury, pardon;*
*Where there is doubt, faith;*
*Where there is despair, hope;*
*Where there is darkness, light;*
*Where there is sadness, joy.*
*O Divine Master,*
*Grant that I may not so much seek*
*To be consoled as to console;*
*To be understood as to understand;*
*To be loved as to love.*
*For it is in giving that we receive;*
*It is in pardoning that we are pardoned;*
*And it is in dying that we are born to eternal life.*
*AMEN*

# Epilogue

EVERYONE LOVES THE PRAYER of St. Francis. It has beautiful words, a delicate poetic embrace, and the ability to summon contentment and peace. It touches us. It moves us. But in my experience, it rarely moves us to action, to a commitment for spiritual formation and holy living. Why? Unfortunately, we often quote this prayer as part of the benediction and just before we head out for a meal. We rarely take time to embrace the power of the prayer, to sit with it and soak it in, and let it speak to us. In other words, we don't practice what we pray. That takes time and intent.

But if we put the Prayer of St. Francis into daily practice, we will find it to be a powerful prayer, dangerous even. It will change our lives. I know it changed mine. Writing this book compelled me to dwell on the spiritual call to sow, seek, and see, to sit with the challenges and changes it bids, and to let them soak in. As I took this prayer seriously, doing my best to practice the prayer every day, I was challenged to love God and neighbor in a new light, in new ways. As it turns out, we do become what we pray.

My prayer is that this book has been helpful to you in seeking to practice the Prayer of St. Francis and that you have been shaped and formed in ways known and unknown by our loving God, who keeps on coming and coming and coming. It's what God does. "And what does the Lord require of you? To act justly and to love mercy and to walk humbly with your God" (Mic 6:8). Justice, mercy, and humility—that sounds like practicing the Prayer of St. Francis to me.

Let's continue to practice this prayer. I suggest that you make one line of this prayer (and the corresponding chapter of the book) an action focus for an entire month. Thus, you can let the prayer speak to you and challenge you throughout the year as you sow, seek, and see in your own neighborhood. In a year's time, who knows what opportunities God will bring your way. Safe travels!

119

# Bibliography

Allen, Patrick. *For Today: A Prayer When Life Gets Messy*. Eugene, OR: Cascade, 2018.
——. *The Good Shepherd, Gentle Guide, and Gracious Host*. Eugene, OR: Cascade, 2020.
——. *Love at Its Best When Church Is a Mess*. Eugene, OR: Cascade, 2020.
Angelou, Maya. "Love Recognizes No Barriers. It Jumps Hurdles, Leaps Fences, Penetrates Walls to Arrive at Its Destination Full of Hope." https://www.goodreads.com/quotes/126888-love-recognizes-no-barriers-it-jumps-hurdles-leaps-fences-penetrates.
Baldwin, James. "Sonny's Blues." In *The Oxford Book of American Short Stories*, edited by Joyce Carol Oates, 409–39. Oxford: Oxford University Press, 2013.
Einstein, Albert. "There Are Only Two Ways to Live Your Life. One Is as Though Nothing Is a Miracle. The Other Is as Though Everything Is." https://quotepark.com/quotes/1362382-albert-einstein-there-are-only-two-ways-to-live-your-life-one-is/.
"For Today." *Forward Day by Day* 88.3 (2022) inside cover.
"Franciscan and Other Prayers." https://www.fspa.org/content/prayer/franciscan-prayers.
Goethe, Wolfgang von. "A Person Hears Only What They Understand." https://www.goalcast.com/johann-wolfgang-von-goethe-quotes/.
Ignatius of Antioch. "The Epistle of Ignatius to the Romans." In Ante-Nicene Fathers, edited by Alexander Roberts et al., vol. 1. Translated by Alexander Roberts and James Donaldson. Buffalo, NY: Christian Literature Publishing Co., 1885. Revised and edited for New Advent by Kevin Knight. https://www.newadvent.org/fathers/0107.htm.
Menninger, Karl A. "Listening Is a Magnetic and Strange Thing, a Creative Force. The Friends Who Listen to Us Are the Ones We Move Toward. When We Are Listened To, It Creates Us, Makes Us Unfold and Expand." https://www.goodreads.com/quotes/442589-listening-is-a-magnetic-and-strange-thing-a-creative-force
Niebuhr, Reinhold. *The Irony of American History*. New York: Charles Scribner's Sons, 1952.
Nouwen, Henri J. M. *Eternal Seasons: A Spiritual Journey through the Church's Year*. Edited by Michael Ford. Notre Dame, IN: Ave Maria Press, 2007.

Made in the USA
Monee, IL
02 November 2022

16966478R00079